Praise for
AIM HIGH
and
BOUNCE BACK

"This book challenges one of the most pervasive myths in modern work—that success means never failing. *Aim High and Bounce Back* exposes how fear of failure quietly drains ambition, particularly for women navigating perfectionism and systemic bias. Drawing on global research and deeply personal stories, Macaulay and Riegel offer a rare combination of data, empathy, and practical wisdom. Their message is both urgent and empowering: Resilience isn't about avoiding failure; it's about redefining it. Every leader—and every organization that values women's leadership—should read this."

—**DAVID SMITH, PHD**; professor and codirector of the Gender & Work Initiative, Johns Hopkins Carey Business School; coauthor, *Good Guys* and *Athena Rising*

"This book reveals what many women experience but rarely discuss: how deeply we internalize failure. More importantly, it provides practical strategies to transform setbacks into stepping stones."

—**DR. TASHA EURICH**, organizational psychologist and *New York Times* best-selling author

"High achievers are often their own harshest critics. Nothing but perfection is allowed, and that is not sustainable if you want to live very long or be very happy. Learn how you and your team can celebrate your beautiful flaws and failures while aiming high and achieving great success. Based on real life stories, this book will teach you how to achieve success at work and at home. You need that; we all do. Find joy in your work again. Read on!"

—**CHESTER ELTON**, executive coach, best-selling author of *The Carrot Principle* and *Leading with Gratitude*

"This work offers a definitive take on the importance, even criticality, of failure as a part of the journey to long-term success. It highlights the often undiscussed, or at least underdiscussed, lessons learned through the hard-fought setbacks that are a universal truth. Examples throughout this captivating book present rare, candid, and inspiring evidence of what it means to get up, dust yourself off, and get back in the arena. I see myself and my stories in these pages, and I look forward to gifting this work to anyone with ambitions and aspirations to do something powerful in the world. Thank you for this much-needed reminder that resilience is not an inherent characteristic; it is a practice, it is a choice, and it defines and fuels our achievements."

—**MARLA BLOW**, CEO and president, Skoll Foundation

"This book transforms our relationship with failure into a powerful tool for growth. It's not just about bouncing back—it's about using setbacks to build the resilience and leadership skills that create lasting impact."

—**FRANCES FREI**, professor, Harvard Business School

"Every woman I've profiled has faced failure on her path to achievement. This book gives you what so many of us need: validation that the obstacles are real, research proving you're not alone, and practical strategies to rise stronger."

—**CAROLINE WATERLOW,**
Academy Award-winning documentary filmmaker

"In today's ever-changing world, resilience is a competitive edge. This book gives leaders a proven framework to bounce back and thrive."

—**ALEX OSTERWALDER,** creator of the Business Model Canvas and Thinkers50 top 10 management thinker

"With rigorous research and deeply practical strategies, *Aim High and Bounce Back* exposes the hidden barriers women face when they stumble and provides a road map for turning setbacks into springboards for success."

—**DORIE CLARK;** executive education faculty, Columbia Business School; Wall Street Journal and *USA Today* best-selling author, *The Long Game*

"Great coaching helps leaders stay curious when setbacks happen. This research-driven book provides the framework that coaches and their clients need to turn failure into fuel for growth."

—**MICHAEL BUNGAY STANIER,**
best-selling author, *The Coaching Habit*

"Building resilient organizations starts with leaders who bounce back authentically from setbacks. This book provides the tools to create cultures where diverse teams lead with purpose and passion through challenges."

—**DR. CINDY PACE**; global culture and engagement leader; adjunct lecturer, Columbia University

AIM HIGH and BOUNCE BACK

A Successful Woman's Guide to
Rethinking and Rising Up from Failure

AIM HIGH and BOUNCE BACK

FIONA M. MACAULAY
DEBORAH GRAYSON RIEGEL

RIVER GROVE
BOOKS

This publication is designed to provide accurate and authoritative information in regard to the subject matter covered. It is sold with the understanding that the publisher and author are not engaged in rendering legal, accounting, or other professional services. Nothing herein shall create an attorney-client relationship, and nothing herein shall constitute legal advice or a solicitation to offer legal advice. If legal advice or other expert assistance is required, the services of a competent professional should be sought.

Published by River Grove Books
Austin, TX
www.rivergrovebooks.com

Copyright © 2026 Fiona M. Macaulay and Deborah Grayson Riegel

All rights reserved.

Thank you for purchasing an authorized edition of this book and for complying with copyright law. No part of this book may be reproduced, stored in a retrieval system, or transmitted by any means, electronic, mechanical, photocopying, recording, or otherwise, without written permission from the copyright holder.

Distributed by River Grove Books

Design and composition by Greenleaf Book Group and Mimi Bark
Cover design by Greenleaf Book Group and Mimi Bark

Publisher's Cataloging-in-Publication data is available.

Print ISBN: 978-1-966629-91-7

eBook ISBN: 978-1-966629-92-4

First Edition

To *Jared*, for reminding me that "good enough" is often perfect.
And to *Arabella* and *Juliet*, who model what it means
to experience both success and setbacks with grace and grit.

To the *WILD leaders* who turned their failures
into fuel and inspired me to write this book.

—Fiona

To *Michael*, *Jacob*, and *Sophie*, who showed me that
my biggest achievements resulted from the courage to fail
combined with the love and support to keep trying.

—Deb

Contents

INTRODUCTION 1

PART 1: Understanding Women's Precarious Relationship with Failure

Chapter 1: Failure—What It Is and Why It Hurts 9

Chapter 2: The Confidence Gap—
A Barrier to Risk-Taking and Leadership 27

Chapter 3: The Perfectionism Trap—
When "Good Enough" Feels Like Failure 35

Chapter 4: The Feedback Problem—
Why Women Don't Get What They Need 45

PART 2: Aim High—Rethinking Your Fear of Failure

Chapter 5: Transforming Your Relationship with Failure 55

Chapter 6: How Entrepreneurs Turn Setbacks into
Strategic Advantages 73

Chapter 7: When the Fear of Failure Peaks—
Navigating the Danger Zone of Doubt 87

Chapter 8: Creating Your Failure-Safe Support System 97

PART 3: Bounce Back

Chapter 9: Ground 109

Chapter 10: Gather 121

Chapter 11: Go! 141

CONCLUSION: From Fearing Failure to Failing Forward 151

ACKNOWLEDGMENTS 153

NOTES 155

ABOUT THE AUTHORS 166

Introduction

FIONA

The heart monitor beeped steadily in the quiet hospital room as I stared at the ceiling tiles. An IV tube snaked from my arm, my chest felt crushed by an invisible weight, and each breath came in shallow, unsatisfying gulps.

The doctor's voice cut through my panicked thoughts. "You're having a panic attack," he said gently. "What are you anxious about?"

The simple answer? Failure.

By twenty-eight years old, I was running a global consulting firm that had just crossed the $1 million mark in annual revenue. On paper, everything looked perfect: I had been named one of the top 1 percent of women business owners in the US by revenue, we were profitable with lots of new business opportunities in our pipeline, and I even had a supportive partner. And yet I lived in fear of my business going belly up and what people would say and think about me.

Of course, there were real stressors. I had consultants working in dangerous conditions in Afghanistan and a very junior staff, and we were all learning this new industry I'd entered. There were always proposals to get out, deadlines to meet, a growing company to manage. But I was obsessed with getting each detail right, everything perfect. The pressure I put on myself was literally eating me alive.

My jaw was constantly clenched, and I'd had two root canals in two years from grinding my teeth at night. I would often lose sleep replaying every detail of the day, imagining everything that could go wrong now, next month, or next year.

The irony was inescapable: The very thing I thought would protect me—my obsession with perfection—was destroying me. I was trapped in a hamster wheel of proving myself, working six and a half days a week because every small setback felt like it could be the end. The success I'd worked so hard to achieve had become a prison where anything less than flawless felt like a failure.

Lying in that hospital bed, with my heart finally slowing to a normal rhythm, I realized something had to change. I couldn't keep living like this.

THE UNIVERSAL EXPERIENCE

If you've ever felt this way, you're not alone. In fact, you're part of a much larger group.

Fiona Macaulay and Deborah Grayson Riegel came together to write this book. Both executive coaches who teach at leading business schools, they bring combined expertise working with thousands of women leaders worldwide. Together, they conducted an original survey of over one thousand women across sixty countries to understand how women experience and recover from professional setbacks.

If reading Fiona's story felt uncomfortably familiar—the physical symptoms of stress, the relentless inner critic, the exhaustion of trying to be perfect—you're experiencing what we discovered is common among ambitious women. The fear of failure isn't just professional anxiety. It becomes a full-body experience that can literally make us sick.

The women who shared their stories with us felt it too. For many leaders, the fear of failure becomes intertwined with identity, worth, and self-acceptance, and this fear can be dangerously costly.

THE GLOBAL REALITY: WHAT 1,000+ WOMEN REVEALED

To better understand how women experience failure in professional settings, in 2024, we conducted a survey on women's relationships with workplace setbacks: 1,063 women across organizational levels and from 60 countries responded to our survey and shared their most intimate experiences with workplace failure. This data has informed every chapter of this book.[1]

Women are clearly ready to break their silence about the fears and setbacks that shape their professional journeys. Their responses paint a revealing picture of the psychological barriers that persist across cultures and career levels and highlight universal patterns in how women internalize failure, fear judgment, and may avoid risk despite their capabilities.

REDEFINING FAILURE: LEARNING FROM THE WOMEN WHO HAVE DONE IT

The hundreds of stories from our survey showed us that not only do women experience multiple types of failure, but we also take it deeply to heart, internalizing failure, blaming ourselves, and struggling to recover. And when the failure wasn't even our fault? That's when it gets really messy. But we realized some of the most successful women in public life we admire have messy failure stories. And more importantly, they found ways to rally again.

This became abundantly clear when Fiona launched the WILD (Women for Impactful Leadership Development) Network's Leadership FailLab, where women can now come together to learn from high-profile women who are willing to share their failures. You'll learn more about the results later in this book.

We've lived through failure ourselves. That's why, throughout this book, we're sharing stories of failure and bouncing back with you: our stories, our friends' stories, vulnerable moments shared by our survey respondents from around the world, and stories of successful women you likely admire. We also asked our colleague Stephanie LeBlanc-Godfrey, former global head of inclusion for women of color at Google, to share specific stories from her own experience as a Black professional woman to directly speak to the additional headwinds women of color face in the United States.

We offer these stories with the hope that they resonate with you, that at least one of these stories connects with the pain or shame you may feel from a failure you've experienced, and that hearing a similar story helps you know you are not alone and inspires you to believe that you, too, can bounce back.

This book is about rethinking our relationship with failure, exploring how different fears hold you back, and shifting toward a healthier, more resilient mindset. Failure doesn't have to signify an end; it can become the foundation of a powerful new beginning.

THE FAILURE MINDSET SHIFT

To help women build a healthier relationship with failure, we've identified seven guiding principles—grounded in research, personal stories, and leadership insights—that will serve as a foundation for forming strategies to bounce back.

1. **Failure hurts—and that's okay:** Failure is a normal (and healthy!) part of the human experience. You're going to fail. It is unavoidable. Some failures are minor setbacks while others have lasting consequences. And especially for high-achieving women, even an isolated failure can come at a high cost. Failure has an emotional impact, and acknowledging the pain is the first step toward resilience.

2. **The fear of failure is often more dangerous than failure itself:** More dreams are killed by fear than by actual failure.

3. **If you think you failed, you failed:** In other words, when it comes to failure, your perception is your reality. The last thing we want you to worry about is, "Am I also failing at defining failure?" Give us a break! As Elizabeth Day writes in her book *How to Fail*, setbacks don't have to be notable in order to be meaningful.[2] They don't have to be public. If we know in our hearts that we let ourselves or someone else down and the memory of this fact comes with a special sting, then go ahead and call it a failure.

4. **Failure is personal—but it's also cultural:** Women, especially minorities, face harsher scrutiny and receive fewer second chances. Understanding the cultural biases around failure is crucial for navigating it.

5. **Failing does not make you a failure:** There's a difference between experiencing a setback and being defined by it. Rethinking failure starts with separating identity from outcomes.

6. **Failure is a leadership skill:** The best leaders don't avoid failure; they prepare for it and learn from it. Leaders who acknowledge mistakes and foster a culture of learning create stronger, more resilient teams.

7. **You can rewire your brain around failure:** Neuroplasticity shows that we can change how we respond to failure. By training ourselves to see failure as a learning opportunity rather than a threat, we build resilience.

These principles set the foundation for recovery from failure, helping you to bounce back and aim high once again.

YOUR ROAD MAP FORWARD

This book is organized into three parts that mirror the journey from fear to resilience:

Part 1: Understanding why failure feels so threatening to women and how systemic barriers shape our experiences.

Part 2: Rethinking your relationship with failure using evidence-based strategies that help you aim high despite uncertainty.

Part 3: Bouncing Back with our Ground, Gather, Go! framework for processing failure, gathering resources, and aiming high again.

You'll also discover why some women navigate setbacks more successfully than others: not because they're more talented but because they've developed specific mental frameworks and support systems that you can learn too.

Failure doesn't have to signify an end. It can become the foundation of a powerful new beginning.

But first, we need to understand why failure feels so dangerous to women in the first place.

By understanding failure through this lens, we can move from fear to action, from hesitation to boldness, and from setbacks to resilience.

Let's fail forward—together.

PART 1

Understanding Women's Precarious Relationship with Failure

Failure hurts. And as women, we need to talk about it—what failure really is and why failure becomes a stake in the heart for so many women.

When failure happens, it can feel like it is all our fault. You may be surprised how many of the painful bumps in the road you've driven through in your career have deep systemic roots.

The research is clear. Women face different consequences for the same mistakes, receive lower-quality feedback, and navigate workplace cultures that punish the very confidence and risk-taking that leadership requires.

The more you understand failure, the better prepared you'll be to deal with it when it inevitably happens to you.

CHAPTER 1

Failure—What It Is and Why It Hurts

DEB

By whatever alchemy of nature and nurture, I have been confident in my abilities for as long as I can remember. Raised in Manhattan, I am a classic fast-talking, fast-thinking, fast-walking New Yorker. Navigating the busy streets of New York, I developed a kind of antenna particular to New Yorkers: I see a small opening in the crowd of people walking in front of me, and I go for it to move forward, faster. I am wired to look for tiny cracks and openings as opportunities.

I got used to being the best, or nearly the best, at everything I did. I was at the top of my class even though I was a year younger than most of my classmates. As eighth grade drew to a close, my classmates and I took an extremely competitive standardized test to see who would get into one of New York's famed specialized science high schools, Stuyvesant High School. All of my closest friends made the cut; I didn't.

I couldn't believe that had happened to me. I was devastated: embarrassed for not acing the exam and humiliated to be ranked below my friends. I'd blown the math section, and my math instructor, my favorite teacher, Mrs. Donner, gave me a great early lesson in failure, starting with a healthy dose of candid tough love: This wasn't something that had just "happened" to me. I was excellent at math, but I simply hadn't studied for the math section of the test as much as I could have. She lightened the moment by teasing me about making her, as my math teacher, look bad. And then she stressed how I could make the most of the situation. Staying at my junior high school for ninth grade was an opportunity to make new friends, try new activities, and even take classes that would boost my GPA, then apply again. I followed Mrs. Donner's advice, had an amazing ninth-grade year, and finished second in my grade. And I finally did get that prized admission into Stuyvesant High School.

Fast-forward a decade, and after completing my master's in social work from Columbia, I founded my own coaching and consulting company, which I've now been running for more than twenty years. I've also published nine books prior to this one. I'm still spotting cracks that lead to opportunities: I see an opening, a hole in the market, and I have an instinct for how to fill it successfully. I've had setbacks that were momentarily devastating (a book proposal that was accepted, until it wasn't; my business tanking during the 2008 financial crisis), but nothing I couldn't bounce back from.

But not all failures are so easy to move past. Some failures feel like a bad test score that stays with you your entire life.

For me, that has been my weight.

Early on, it seemed like my weight issues would be my own personal glass ceiling. When I was five years old, I asked my first-grade classmates if I could be in their "lip gloss club." My enthusiastic interest was met with a terse "Maybe if you lose fifty pounds." First grade. Five years old.

This led to more than four decades of overeating, dieting, and overexercising to compensate. I developed an eating disorder that included an exercise routine that has led to permanent injuries and a shame-based relationship with food. I had a keen awareness of how much space my body was physically taking up, as well as how much space this issue was taking up in my brain. Yet I felt powerless to change it.

Some failures are external—a setback that forces you to pivot. That was my Stuyvesant rejection. It hurt, but I could course-correct and move forward.

But other failures become part of your identity. They don't feel like moments that happened to you; they feel like reflections of who you are. That's what my weight struggle felt like—an inescapable failure that shaped how I saw myself.

When someone met me for the first time, I always anticipated that initial impression, that snap judgment, immediately assessing me as a failure in this one thing. I compensated with humor and expertise, anything to distract people from this visible failure I carried. It was exhausting.

Then I realized something remarkable. Although the specter of failing at this one thing has hung over me my entire life, I got everything I ever could have wanted: an amazing career, a great marriage, and wonderful kids. So what was the big deal about being in a bigger body?

After years of trying to reconcile this on my own, I reached out to a therapist to help me make sense of this cognitive dissonance: For all the ways I had succeeded, I was still carrying around the belief that I had failed.

I made the hardest pivot I've ever had to make: Instead of investing energy in distraction and deflection, I would invest it in acknowledging my feelings and normalizing my response. I realized that just about every woman has something hanging over her, some hidden glass ceiling she is afraid of bumping up against. Many women wrestle with that lingering fear: "What if, for all my apparent successes and gifts, they find out X about me?"

I've decided to shift from "What if?" to "Even if..."

- *What if I fail?* → Even if I fail, I'll keep going.
- *What if they judge me?* → Even if they judge me, I'll still show up.

FAILURE IS UBIQUITOUS

The difference between people who thrive through failure and those who get stuck isn't the absence of failure; it's how they process and respond to it. You've already proven you can do this. The small failures you navigate daily without thinking twice? That's evidence of your existing resilience.

The goal isn't to avoid failure; that's impossible. The goal is to expand your definition of what's manageable. If you can handle the everyday setbacks without calling them failures, you can learn to handle the bigger ones too.

WHAT WE MEAN BY FAILURE

While in the ER, Fiona realized that her fear wasn't just about failure; it was about not even understanding what failure really meant to her. Was she failing because she wasn't perfect? Because she felt overwhelmed? Because others might judge her? Our research revealed that this confusion about failure itself is part of what can make it so paralyzing.

But here's what we learned from women who trusted us with their most vulnerable moments in our global survey about women's experiences with failure: Understanding your failure pattern is the first step to changing it.[1]

From our survey, we identified five types of failure experiences that shape how we navigate risk, ambition, and recovery: concrete failure, circumstantial failure, perceived failure, identity failure, and paralysis failure. Understanding which type you're facing or fearing is the first step toward changing your relationship with failure itself.

As you read these five types, pay attention to which one makes your stomach tighten or your heart race faster. That physical response is telling you something important about your own failure patterns.

When the Numbers Don't Lie: Concrete Failure

For most of us, failure is something we had great hopes for but that worked out badly. We aim high for something and either come up short or miss entirely. Because the outcome stands in such sharp contrast to our hopes and expectations, these failures can really gut us.

You'll know you're experiencing this when there's a clear metric that shows you didn't meet specific goals. Concrete failure looks like not getting the promotion despite your track record. Or the product launch you've been planning for months falls flat. Or your carefully crafted proposal gets rejected. These failures sting because the metrics are crystal clear: You either made it or you didn't.

What really struck us in the responses to our global survey was how women described the sharp pain of missing measurable targets, especially when they'd done everything "right." As one respondent shared, "I hit every KPI except the one that mattered." This pattern showed up repeatedly—women feeling the sharp sting of missing concrete targets despite flawless execution.

These failures sting because the metrics are clear and unmet, but they're also the easiest to learn from and move past.

When Life Happens to You: Circumstantial Failure

This is the failure that blindsides you. Someone else creates the mess, but you're left cleaning it up. Working for a toxic boss destroys your confidence. Your business partner makes decisions that tank the company. A family crisis derails years of careful planning. You didn't cause the problem, but somehow you're the one who feels like a failure.

You'll know you're experiencing this when you find yourself thinking, "This isn't my fault, but I'm paying the price." This came up over and over in survey responses: women trapped in situations they didn't create but couldn't escape from.

> FIONA
>
> I recently coached a woman who stepped into a nonprofit already hemorrhaging money—a reality that had been hidden from her during the hiring process. Staff were demoralized after two failed turnaround attempts, and a major funding deadline loomed just nine months away.
>
> She worked seventy-hour weeks rebuilding trust while making painful but necessary cuts. Slowly, the team began to believe in her vision.
>
> New board members had joined in the meantime. They hadn't been part of the original decision to hire her. Donors grew nervous. The standard for success kept shifting.
>
> Then a key donor pulled out unexpectedly, and the board panicked.
>
> She brought the budget within striking distance of balance and secured commitments to replace the lost funding. It wasn't enough. The board fired her for "insufficient progress" and hired a man to implement the exact turnaround plan she had created.

Our key insight for circumstantial failure is that it is crucial to recognize when failure stems from factors beyond your control so that you can protect your self-worth and make strategic decisions about what to do next.

When the World Calls It Wrong: Perceived Failure

There are times when the world calls a decision a failure even though you know you made the right choice—like when headlines label you "quitting" when instead you're quietly protecting your sanity, your values, or your future. Critics call it giving up, but you understand it as strategic self-preservation. When others judge your decision harshly, but you feel aligned with your values, you'll know you're experiencing perceived failure.

This type of failure showed up in our survey when women talked about leaving toxic jobs without backup plans or walking away from relationships that looked perfect from the outside. As one respondent said, "Everyone thought I was crazy for leaving, but I finally felt sane."

Sometimes it's not leaving a job; it's stepping back from an assignment or project for *your* right reasons. One respondent had worked closely with local scriptwriters to help create a radio drama series in Rwanda. But living there for over a year, far from her now husband, proved tough, and she decided to leave. The project continued and was a real success, broadcasting on national radio. Reflecting on her decision, she said, "I learned that sometimes my own personal needs have to come first."

We loved the perspective of yet another young professional, who had unsuccessfully run for president of Paraguay: "It was not a failure for me; it was a learning experience. I demonstrated that young people have a voice and vote and that we can make a difference in politics."

Sometimes what looks like failure to others is actually the brave choice that aligns with your authentic self.

> **WHEN SUCCESS LOOKS LIKE FAILURE TO THE OUTSIDE WORLD[2]**
>
> Stephanie Cohen had built what most would consider the ultimate career. After almost twenty-five years at Goldman Sachs, she sat on the Management Committee as one of the most senior women

continued

at the firm. She ran consumer and wealth management, had been chief strategy officer, and was widely recognized as a powerhouse in investment banking. To the outside world, she had everything—prestige, influence, and a clear path to even greater heights.

But at forty-seven, Stephanie found herself asking different questions: Where could she have the most impact? How could she affect the world her kids live in? The answer led her away from Goldman Sachs and toward technology.

When she announced she was taking a sabbatical, the reactions were swift and predictable. "Why would you leave? That's what everyone who walks in the door there wants," people said. "How could you just walk away from it?" Some colleagues assumed Goldman Sachs must be "impossible for women" and wanted that narrative to explain her departure.

The truth was more nuanced. "It wasn't about whether you can be senior and successful at Goldman Sachs as a woman," Stephanie reflected. "It wasn't about whether staying at Goldman Sachs is a good idea. It was about me." She needed to figure out who she was beyond the identity she'd held for twenty-five years—longer than any other relationship except her immediate family.

The sabbatical itself was initially miserable. "The first month was kind of awful because it's like detox," she explained. "Your whole way of operating is used to a certain thing that entirely goes away." She avoided anyone who wanted to discuss her career choices, speaking only to family for the first month.

What looked like failure to many—walking away from the pinnacle of financial services success—was actually strategic self-preservation and authentic career evolution. When she eventually joined Cloudflare, a company that helps keep websites secure and running quickly by routing and protecting internet traffic at a global scale, as chief strategy officer, some people finally understood. "There were certain people who would say, 'I talked to you three years ago. This is not surprising at all because you had decided that the world was being driven by everything happening in technology.'"

Stephanie's story illustrates the courage required to redefine success on your own terms, even when the world can't understand why you'd leave what they see as the ultimate achievement. Sometimes the bravest choice is the one that looks like failure to everyone else.

When You Lose Yourself in the Process: Identity Failure

Failure that chips away at your identity cuts deep. You wake up one day and realize you've become someone you don't recognize. Maybe you're successful by every external measure but feel completely hollow inside. You've compromised your values so often that you've lost sight of what matters to you. The failure isn't about missing a goal; it's about missing yourself. When success feels empty and you don't like who you've become in pursuit of it, you'll know you're experiencing identity failure.

This showed up constantly, particularly among high-achieving women who felt disconnected from who they used to be. As one respondent put it, "I became someone I didn't recognize or like. I was impatient, controlling, and lost my empathy and grace. I became hard and demanding because I thought that's what it took to get results. I realized I had lost myself completely in trying to achieve this goal."

Stories like this taught us something important: We don't need to abandon our ambitions, but we do need to listen to signals that we should realign our methods with our values.

When Fear Wins Before You Start: Paralysis Failure

When you stop yourself from trying for something big, that's paralysis failure. It's the promotion you never applied for because you weren't "ready yet." It's the business idea you've been perfecting but still haven't launched. It's the conversation you keep putting off until the "right moment" that never comes. If you find yourself endlessly preparing but never starting, you'll know you're experiencing paralysis failure.

This kind of failure isn't about trying and missing the mark. It's about being so afraid of concrete failure that you choose certain stagnation instead. One of our survey respondents captured it perfectly: "I became so good at avoiding failure that I also avoided success."

Which of these failure types sounds most familiar? Most women experience two or three of these patterns. There's no wrong answer; this is just your starting point for change.

THE LEADERSHIP FAILLAB: WHERE SUCCESSFUL WOMEN SHARE THEIR SETBACKS

When Fiona introduced the WILD Network's Leadership FailLab, she was addressing something missing from traditional leadership development forums. Unlike conventional leadership seminars that focus on polished success stories, the FailLab was designed to normalize failure as an essential leadership skill. The format was deliberately different: Speakers would share their most devastating professional setbacks in front of hundreds of people, including clients, vendors, and their employees.

What emerged surprised everyone. As Fiona watched CEO after CEO (women running companies worth hundreds of millions and the world's most highly regarded not-for-profit organizations and leaders who'd won industry awards) courageously share their failures, she witnessed something transformative: They weren't crushed by their mistakes. They were confident enough to broadcast their screwups publicly, and in doing so, they were creating something revolutionary.

Fiona discovered a specific formula that encouraged genuine vulnerability rather than surface-level inspiration. For the FailLab to work, speakers needed three essential elements: Establish success credentials so the audience knew these were accomplished leaders, be ruthlessly honest about the failure with specific details of what went wrong, and extract concrete lessons learned that others could apply.

This combination of proven success plus specific failure created something magical. When audiences saw accomplished leaders sharing detailed accounts of their setbacks, it gave everyone permission to be human. A US nonprofit leader confronted her blind spots around unconscious bias, sharing how her good intentions masked harmful assumptions that damaged relationships with the communities she served. Her story illustrated identity failure: the painful realization that her actions contradicted her values.

A Ghanaian executive living with a disability spoke about redefining herself beyond societal expectations of disability, describing years of paralysis failure during which fear of judgment kept her from pursuing leadership roles she was qualified for. Her breakthrough came when she realized that the cost of playing it safe exceeded the risk of being visible.

A Colombian entrepreneur shared her battle with chronic burnout, detailing how she had achieved every external marker of success while feeling completely hollow inside. Her experience of identity failure led her to redefine success on her own terms, prioritizing well-being alongside achievement.

Through the FailLab, Fiona came to understand how much fear of failure people carried and how talking about it openly was liberating for leaders at all stages of their careers. She witnessed firsthand that failure wasn't the end of the leadership journey but rather an integral part of it. The transformations she saw in the audience members after each session revealed that normalizing failure was part of professional growth and could unlock potential that fear had kept hidden.

WHY FAILURE FEELS LIKE A THREAT

Failure feels like a threat because our brains are wired for survival. Our brains process failure the same way they process physical pain.[3] This response made sense in ancient times—being cast out of a group could mean life or death. But today, this instinct causes us to react to setbacks as if they're existential threats, even when they're not.

But here's what makes failure especially painful for women: It's not just about the immediate consequences. When we fail, we don't just think, "This didn't work." We think, "What does this say about who I am?"

Women in general are more likely to internalize failure as a reflection of their abilities while men tend to externalize it as a factor of circumstance.[4] This leads to greater self-doubt and a reluctance to take risks in their careers. Research shows the following:

- Women are more likely to attribute failure to a lack of ability while men more frequently attribute failure to external factors, like bad luck or circumstances beyond their control.[5]
- Women prone to perfectionism tend to play it safe, which holds them back from advancement.
- Female leaders face harsher scrutiny for failure than their male counterparts, making setbacks feel even riskier.[6]

These biases don't just shape how the world sees us; they shape how we see ourselves. This fear of the reputational cost of failure is why women tend to hesitate before applying for promotions, negotiate for raises less frequently, and take fewer public risks.

When we experience failure—whether a rejected job application, a lost client, or a public mistake—our brains interpret it as social rejection. The amygdala, our brains' threat detection system, goes into overdrive, activating the fight-or-flight response. This is why failure can feel so emotionally overwhelming.

Are we really the person, the leader, the colleague, the friend we intend and aspire to be?

There is good news. While our brains are wired to see failure as dangerous, we can train ourselves to respond differently.

DEB

WHY WOMEN INTERNALIZE FAILURE MORE DEEPLY

I remember walking into my office one day and finding a Post-it note with "see me" written on it in my supervisor's handwriting. In a flash,

I'd decided that "see me" meant "you're fired." In the thirty-second walk down the hall to my manager's office, I had mentally updated my resume, told my husband that I'd been let go, and planned how I would share the terrible news with my friends and colleagues. Needless to say, I was not fired. I don't even remember what the "see me" conversation was about. I did, however, request that my boss not leave Post-it notes like that again.

FROM CONTRIBUTOR STEPHANIE LEBLANC-GODFREY
THE LONELY "ONLY"

Women of color often have the added burden of being the "Only"—the sole person of their race or ethnicity in meetings, departments, or leadership roles.

Recent data shows this isolation remains widespread: 46 percent of Black women, 41 percent of Latina women, and 42 percent of Asian women report frequently being the only person of their background in professional settings.[7]

From my personal experience, I would add another way that being an Only takes a toll on women of color: sheer exhaustion. It is simply exhausting for us to keep aiming high. As we are doing so, we are wondering, "Am I enough?" or asking ourselves, "How big do I dream?" There is even more exhaustion in getting a promotion or a stretch assignment and then feeling our job or career or reputation could be on the line, because if we stumble, the failure likely won't be written off as a learning moment, and we fear we could be dismissed as one and done.

Women of color face additional pressure in which individual mistakes reflect on entire groups. This creates rational caution that can be misinterpreted as lack of confidence or ambition.

Women of color deal with unique internal headwinds in the form of inherited cultural assumptions about how we should or should not act and about the personal price we must pay to attain success. Obviously, there is a rich array of cultural traditions that inform the lives of women of color, and I don't want to paint this picture with too broad of a brush. But there are some common elements:

- The idea that you have to work twice as hard and be twice as good
- The "keep your head down until you've arrived" mentality
- The feeling that you're not just striving on your own behalf but also on behalf of others of your race or gender who may come after you—so failure simply isn't an option

According to the *2021 US Women of Color in Business: Cross-Generational Survey*, 32 percent of Black women (twice the number of white women) feel their race and/or gender makes people view their work with skepticism and scrutiny. (Those figures are 25 percent for Latina women and 21 percent for Asian women.)[8]

The organizational headwinds women face are compounded when women are the only representative of their ethnicity, race, or identity. They can be subject to great scrutiny, are given few stretch assignments, and receive limited feedback and mentoring.[9]

But even beyond the question of feedback, an Only needs space—mental space and temporal space—in which to absorb lessons, consider options, and proactively plan her career. That room to pause and breathe is rare and precious for all employees in an "always on" corporate culture. And it seems particularly rare for women of color, who are squeezed by commitments outside of work, the constant pressure to go above and beyond and be overprepared, and the need to devote more (unpaid!) time to the unofficial work of educating colleagues and supervisors about inclusion and support in the workplace.

WHEN FAILURE BECOMES IDENTITY: THE PSYCHOLOGY BEHIND THE SHIFT

Do any of these internal statements of doubt sound familiar?

"I didn't just mess up that presentation; I'm bad at public speaking."

"I didn't just lose that client; I'm terrible at my job."

"I didn't just make a wrong decision; I'm not cut out for leadership."

Our feelings about failure become detrimental when failure stops being something we experience and instead becomes something we believe we are. This shift from external event to internal identity happens through specific psychological processes. When we experience failure, our brains struggle with what psychologists call cognitive dissonance—the uncomfortable tension between who we think we are and what just happened.[10]

Failure, by itself, is just a setback. But when we attach it to our self-worth, it turns into shame—which is far more destructive. Researcher and author Brené Brown describes shame as "the intensely painful feeling or experience of believing we are flawed and therefore unworthy of love, belonging, and connection."[11] Shame doesn't just say, *You failed.* It says, *You are a failure.* Internalizing that message prompts us to make choices not in our best interest:

- We hold ourselves back from future risks
- We overcompensate, working twice as hard to prove ourselves
- We stay silent about our struggles, reinforcing the belief that everyone else is succeeding except us

But here's the truth: Failure is an event. It is not an identity.

THE COST OF PLAYING IT SAFE

We discovered a troubling pattern: Roughly one in five women (21 percent of survey respondents) explicitly admitted to risk-averse behavior that was actively limiting their career advancement.

As one respondent said, "I have strongly avoided taking risks, opting for things that I know I will be successful at in order to maintain my confidence." Another reflected with painful honesty: "I tend to play it safe when it comes to my career progression, which has caused me to reach my milestones much later than expected."

This risk aversion showed up in concrete ways across our survey responses:

- Declining stretch assignments because of perceived expertise gaps
- Avoiding presentations because of concerns about language fluency
- Staying silent in meetings rather than risk being wrong
- Applying to the same leadership program multiple times before feeling "ready"

What makes this particularly damaging is that women's risk aversion often stems from perfectionism rather than genuine inability. They're not avoiding challenges because they can't handle them. They're avoiding them because they can't guarantee perfect performance.

The irony is stark: In trying to protect their confidence by only pursuing sure wins, these women were systematically undermining the very confidence they sought to preserve.

The pattern creates a vicious cycle. By avoiding risks, women miss opportunities to build resilience, expand their capabilities, and develop the tolerance for uncertainty that leadership requires.

The most successful women we know have learned to reframe risk entirely. Instead of seeing uncertainty as a threat to their competence, they viewed it as evidence they were pushing themselves toward growth. They understand that feeling unprepared wasn't a signal to retreat; it was a signal they were heading in the right direction.

Key Takeaways

- **Separate failure from identity:** When you catch yourself saying, "I am a failure," stop and rephrase it as, "I failed at something." This simple change protects your identity.
- **Start small:** Note the minor disappointments you handle every day without calling them failures. You're already more resilient than you think.
- **Identify your failure pattern:** Which of the five failure types (concrete, circumstantial, perceived, identity, or paralysis) feels most familiar? Understanding your pattern is the first step to changing it.

CHAPTER 2

The Confidence Gap— A Barrier to Risk-Taking and Leadership

Christine Lagarde, the first woman to lead both the International Monetary Fund (IMF) and the European Central Bank, spent much of her career navigating male-dominated spaces. Despite her extensive background in finance and law, she was often underestimated, overlooked, and questioned in ways her male counterparts were not.[1]

When she was first approached about taking the top position at the IMF, Christine hesitated. "I remember thinking, 'Am I the right person for this?'" she later recalled. "I had all the qualifications, but I wasn't sure I was ready."

Her male competitors, however, had no such hesitation. They put their names forward without questioning their own readiness—even those with significantly less experience than her.

Ultimately, Christine took the role and led the IMF through one of the most turbulent financial crises in modern history, proving herself to be not only capable but also exceptional. Looking back, she noted,

"Too often, women doubt themselves when they should not. I have learned that if an opportunity comes your way, say yes, even before you feel ready."

THE REAL PROBLEM: CONSEQUENCES, NOT CONFIDENCE

Christine's story underscores a critical truth that has been misunderstood for decades. What we call the confidence gap—the idea that women hesitate to seek opportunities because of self-doubt, popularized by Katty Kay and Claire Shipman in *The Confidence Code*[2]—isn't actually about confidence at all. It's about consequences. Here's what researchers discovered when they dug deeper: Women are just as confident as men but face different social penalties for demonstrating it. Women who self-promote are more likely to be judged as too aggressive or not likable enough. Meanwhile, men are more likely to be overconfident, attributing success to their abilities and failure to external factors.[3] Rather than a *confidence* gap, the real issue is often a *consequence* gap—where women are penalized when behaving in ways for which men are rewarded.

This helps explain why even accomplished professionals—executives, entrepreneurs, directors, and senior managers who have already proven their capabilities—still struggle with self-doubt. Women tend to be more accurate than men when assessing their own capabilities, but in environments that reward bold risk-taking, this can work against them.[4] The disconnect between their actual competence and their internal experience reveals how systemic barriers can undermine even successful women's willingness to take risks or pursue advancement opportunities.

WHERE STRATEGIC CAUTION STARTS: THE DEVELOPMENT PIPELINE

To understand how this consequence gap develops, we need to trace its origins through a girl's development. This consequence gap has deep roots. By age six, girls learn that brilliance belongs to others while perfect execution belongs to them.[5] School reinforces this pattern. Girls develop what researcher Lisa Damour calls "inefficient overwork," feeling unsafe without maximum effort, while boys learn strategic risk-taking.[6] When 43 percent of girls abandon sports because of fear of judgment, they lose crucial resilience-building opportunities that boys continue accessing.[7] These early patterns create adults who've been trained to avoid rather than navigate failure and crystallize into workplace realities where women's strategic caution is misinterpreted as lack of confidence.

Nobody's sitting in staff meetings plotting how to hold girls back. Teachers and administrators aren't doing this on purpose. They're passing on what they absorbed growing up—the same messages about what girls and boys are supposed to be good at. A girl gets praised for her neat handwriting and following directions carefully. A boy gets encouragement to try a bold approach, even if it's messy. Same classroom, different messages.

THE WORKPLACE REALITY: WHEN CONSEQUENCES AREN'T EQUAL

The perception that women lack confidence has led to widespread assumptions about their willingness to take risks. For example, studies have suggested that women are more risk-averse, particularly in finance and investing.[8] However, recent research challenges this narrative. Women are not inherently more risk-averse; rather, they are just as attuned to the consequences of failure in the financial sphere as they are in other professional and personal circumstances.[9]

Research reveals the stark reality of unequal consequences. When male and female executives make the same mistake, women are penalized more harshly in performance reviews and less likely to get opportunities for recovery.[10] For example, female surgeons face greater reputational damage for medical errors compared to male surgeons, leading to fewer referrals and diminished career prospects.[11] The pattern is clear: identical mistakes, unequal consequences.

THE GLASS CLIFF

Companies in crisis are significantly more likely to hand leadership roles to women, meaning female leaders face a higher probability of failure simply because of when they step in. A 2016 study confirmed this pattern, finding women are more likely to be promoted to CEO roles during financial crisis, setting them up for greater scrutiny and risk.

These situations are failure traps disguised as opportunities. You inherit a failing division, a demoralized team, and unrealistic expectations for a quick turnaround. When things don't improve immediately, guess who gets blamed?

This pattern of setting women up to fail creates the perfect conditions for another problem: the double standard of failure.

DEB
THE DOUBLE STANDARD OF FAILURE

When I experience a failure, I worry about the impact it might have on other subgroups I represent. Will my failure make it harder for working mothers? Jewish women? Female entrepreneurs? This set of concerns can contribute to both rumination about failure and hiding failures, both of which I am committed to reversing.

Deb's worries aren't born in a vacuum. When women do fail or are perceived to have failed, their stories are told very differently than when men do. Here's how the double standard actually works.

Just look at female CEOs. When companies fail under women's leadership, guess who gets blamed? A Rockefeller Foundation report found that when the leader was a woman, nearly 80 percent of media stories singled her out as a source of blame. When the leader was a man, only 31 percent identified him as the culprit. In stories about male CEOs of troubled companies, gender usually never comes up (it is mentioned only 4 percent of the time). In cases when the troubled company is headed by a woman, her gender is mentioned 49 percent of the time.[12]

It's not just CEOs either. This punishment gap shows up everywhere. In financial services, women caught in misconduct were 20 percent more likely than a man to be fired and 30 percent less likely to find new employment in the industry.[13] In health care, female surgeons are punished more than men for the same mistake.[14]

Black women leaders in the United States in particular suffer from a kind of double jeopardy in which they are blamed and sanctioned more when organizations fail but also get less credit when they succeed.[15]

FIONA

The head pat happened during what should have been one of the proudest moments of my career up to that point. It was early days of my first social venture; I was twenty-eight, sitting in a conference room in Washington, DC, about to sign a large contract—the biggest deal my global consulting firm had ever landed. This opportunity had come from taking a number of calculated risks and investments of time and money I didn't have to build an impressive track record of project implementation in French-speaking African countries.

As I reached for the pen to sign the contract, one of the senior executives reached over and patted me on the head—like I was his daughter who'd just brought home a good report card.

The room went silent. The other young professionals at the table stared at me in horror. My feelings of pride, confidence, and achievement drained from my body and in a split second were replaced with feeling like a little girl being bestowed a favor.

Later that week, at an industry conference, a keynote speaker—a woman I'd admired and hoped to connect with—dismissed me before I could even introduce myself properly. When I mentioned my work helping communities in Africa build sustainable businesses, she looked me up and down and said, "I've never seen anything good come out of Africa." Then she turned her back and walked away.

As she left, my mind raced: Was she trying to signal that young innovators weren't welcome in the industry? Had I been fooling myself about the value of our work? Maybe I really was just a naive, well-meaning entrepreneur who didn't understand the complexities of global development.

Sometimes, the simple act of taking a seat at the table was seen as an infraction. In another meeting with potential partners, two mid-level managers spent thirty minutes discussing their golf games and weekend hiking trips while I sat there with my presentation materials, checking my watch. Finally, one said, "Well, we should wrap this up. Our boss said we had to meet with you, so . . . meeting done."

Each moment felt like a small cut that never quite healed. I'd lie awake replaying these interactions, wondering what I'd done wrong. Was I not assertive enough? Too young looking? Not credible enough? Some mornings I'd wake up with my jaw aching from clenching my teeth all night.

What looked like a *confidence* gap was actually a *consequence* gap. When men my age made bold moves or took up space in meetings, they were seen as natural leaders. When I did the same things, I was patted on the head or dismissed entirely.

The real tragedy wasn't that I lacked confidence; it was that I started to question myself in a system designed to make me do exactly that.

A study found that when risk-taking opportunities resulted in equal consequences for men and women, gender differences in risk-taking disappeared.[16] This suggests that women are not *afraid* of risk but rather *strategic* about when and how they take risks.

Our own survey confirmed this caution. The women we surveyed spoke of fear of being judged by peers if they fail, of being held to unrealistic expectations, and of their reputation being harmed. Said one respondent, "I feared the failure of being pushed out and having my reputation damaged like the previous manager in my role." Another admitted that she sometimes didn't speak up at work because of the fear of "being looked at by managers and peers as a failure or being demeaned or shamed by a manager."[17]

REFRAMING THE SOLUTION

Here's the bottom line: The problem isn't that women lack confidence. It's that they lack the freedom to display confidence without facing consequences. What appear to be hesitations are actually strategic calculations.

When the risk assessments women make (either deliberately or reflexively) about whether to aim high are misdiagnosed as lack of confidence, that inappropriately places the burden of change on individual women. Instead, what are crucially needed are effective strategies that address the root causes of many failures: the systemic barriers women face. The solution isn't teaching women to be more confident; it's creating environments where confident behavior is rewarded equally regardless of gender:

- For organizations: Instead of confidence training, organizations need bias training for managers.
- For women: Instead of teaching women to lean in, create inclusive cultures in which all voices are heard. Instead of telling people to take more risks, create systems in which risks and rewards are distributed equally.

Understanding that the confidence gap is actually a consequence gap changes everything. It shifts focus from fixing women to fixing systems. When we create workplaces where confident behavior is rewarded equally regardless of gender, we'll finally see what women can achieve without having to choose between success and acceptance.

Key Takeaways

- **Recognize the real issue:** Women don't lack competence; they face systemic barriers that punish confident behavior and limit opportunities for advancement.

- **Challenge the confidence narrative:** When you hesitate before taking a risk, ask yourself whether you're being strategic or scared. The confidence gap often masks deeper problems, like unequal access to networks and harsher consequences for the same mistakes.

- **Understand the development pipeline:** Girls are conditioned from early childhood to avoid risk and seek perfection, creating patterns that follow them into their careers.

CHAPTER 3

The Perfectionism Trap— When "Good Enough" Feels Like Failure

Brené Brown built her career on studying vulnerability and courage. Yet for years, she struggled with the very thing she later taught others to overcome: perfectionism.

As a young academic, Brené found herself caught in the trap of believing that her work had to be flawless before she could share it. She obsessed over research findings, edited and reedited papers to exhaustion, and hesitated to speak up in professional settings unless she felt completely prepared. To her, success meant eliminating every possible flaw before allowing her ideas into the world.[1]

This relentless self-criticism stalled her career and stifled her confidence. It wasn't until she began researching vulnerability that she had a revelation: Perfectionism is not about striving for excellence; it's about avoiding failure.

Brené realized that her pursuit of perfection was actually fear in disguise—the fear of criticism, of not being good enough, or of being exposed as inadequate—all responses to perceived failure. Her breakthrough came when she chose to publicly embrace imperfection. She took the risk of sharing unpolished work, giving talks in which she spoke candidly about self-doubt, and allowing herself to be seen—flaws and all.

One of her biggest leaps of faith was delivering her now-famous TED Talk on vulnerability. She almost didn't release it, worried it wasn't perfect. But when she let go of that fear, the talk resonated with millions, catapulting her into the global spotlight as a thought leader on courage and authenticity.

Today, Brené teaches that perfectionism doesn't make us stronger; it makes us smaller. It keeps us from taking risks, speaking up, and stepping into leadership. As she puts it, "Perfectionism is not about self-improvement; it's about trying to earn approval. Great leaders are willing to be seen as they are—imperfect, but courageous."

DEB
THE HIGH PRICE OF PERFECTION

I was a perfectionist as a teenager. I'd study for exams well into the night or turn in third, fourth, or even fifth drafts of assignments when others were submitting their first. On one hand, this drive helped me achieve the high GPA and multiple awards across school subjects that fueled my sense of accomplishment. On the other hand, it contributed to sleepless nights, debilitating anxiety, and a painful tic in my neck that I'm still recovering from today, decades later. I now consider myself an antiperfectionist, having paid the perfection tax for so many years. I find my new comfort zone in 80 percent success, getting the B+, and producing in lieu of perfecting.

FIONA

Growing up, my parents focused heavily on my weaknesses, rarely acknowledging my successes. Poor math grades on an otherwise stellar report card became the central topic of conversation at home for days (years!), yet when I landed the lead in a school play or brought home ribbons from gymnastics competitions, those achievements went unrecognized.

Six years into running my first company, I identified a gap that demanded action: a global platform connecting professionals involved in the work of linking low-income youth to career opportunities. I took a bold step by launching the first-ever global summit on the issue, an undertaking typically reserved for large global institutions like the World Bank or the United Nations.

At home, my husband often heard me anxiously reviewing every detail. He made me a tile wall hanging that said "Good Enough." Ironically, all I could see were its imperfections: the rough edges and uneven spacing. I couldn't bring myself to display it. My relentless drive for flawlessness often overshadowed the joy that might have come from the creativity, boldness, and success that made my work impactful in the first place. As Brené puts it, perfectionism is "a 20-ton shield that we lug around, thinking it will protect us, when in fact, it's the thing preventing us from being seen."[2]

When I eventually sold my company for seven figures, it freed me. Looking back, I realized I had developed those perfectionist tendencies in response to the confidence hits I'd taken as an ambitious young woman. In response, I falsely assumed that being flawless would protect me. Even as the company flourished, those habits remained deeply ingrained. Stepping away from the company allowed me to abandon perfectionism and readily accept setbacks.

This shift freed me to embrace what I'd been running from. The journey taught me that there's a crucial difference between pursuing excellence and falling into the trap of perfectionism. Excellence drives and propels you forward; perfectionism paralyzes you with obsession, leads to endless self-punishment, and ultimately becomes an act of self-sabotage. I still value quality deeply, but I've learned to recognize when my standards are serving me versus when they're destroying me. Today, I proudly display the perfectly imperfect "Good Enough" art on my office wall.

THE PERFECTIONISM SPECTRUM

Children raised in environments where affection hinges on achievement often believe their worth is tied directly to flawless performance, fueling lifelong anxiety and fear of failure.[3] These individuals internalize the belief that mistakes equal unworthiness, driving them to pursue unattainable standards in adulthood.

This is especially true for high achievers. In our experience, many executives, entrepreneurs, and leaders grew up receiving praise primarily for their accomplishments rather than for their efforts or character. Deb was consistently praised by parents and teachers alike for her wins rather than for her efforts, so when something required her to struggle a bit, she was more likely to quit than to persevere. Being recognized mainly for our wins fosters a deep-seated fear of failure, making the person more likely to equate self-worth with performance.

Additionally, neuroscientists have linked perfectionism to heightened activity in the anterior cingulate cortex, the brain's error-monitoring system. This hyperactivity can cause individuals to fixate on mistakes, fueling excessive self-criticism.[4] While Deb's parents encouraged her to succeed, they never rebuked her if she didn't; her sense of shame was entirely self-generated. In other words, some people are wired to be more sensitive to imperfections, leading to a relentless pursuit of flawlessness.

Perfectionism doesn't affect everyone the same way, and not all perfectionism is harmful. Psychologists differentiate between adaptive perfectionism, which drives high standards without debilitating self-criticism, and maladaptive perfectionism, which links self-worth to unattainable ideals.

- **Adaptive perfectionism** fuels persistence, creativity, and ambition. It helps individuals set high goals and work toward them with resilience.
- **Maladaptive perfectionism** is driven by fear—fear of failure, of disappointing others, or of not measuring up. It leads to procrastination, burnout, and an inability to celebrate achievements.

PERFECTIONISM, CULTURE, AND WOMEN

For some women, the shift from adaptive to maladaptive perfectionism begins early. Studies show that by middle school, girls tend to internalize the belief that intelligence and ability are innate traits rather than skills that can be developed.[5] This fixed mindset makes failure feel like a referendum on their worth rather than a stepping stone to growth.

For all young people, there is concern that perfectionism is a growing societal phenomenon. A landmark study found that rates of perfectionism have been rising steadily since the 1980s, particularly in Western societies. Their analysis of 41,641 college students over three decades revealed that perfectionism has increased in every form: the impossible standards we set for ourselves, the pressure we feel from others to be perfect, and the harsh judgments we place on everyone around us, largely due to growing cultural expectations for success and the rise of social media.[6]

Social media has exacerbated the issue by creating an environment where curated perfection is the norm. In the fall of 2023, forty-one states and the District of Columbia filed suit against Meta, the owner of both Facebook and Instagram, charging the company and its platforms with intentionally designing them with features that harm teens and other young users, especially girls. Instagram, with its photo editing and photo filtering functions, is seen as especially dangerous for teen girls' body image and overall well-being. A *Wall Street Journal* report, drawing on documents provided by a whistleblower, shows that the company was for years well aware of these effects, even as they publicly downplayed the issue.[7]

Kara Alaimo's book *Over the Influence: Why Social Media Is Toxic for Women and Girls—and How We Can Take It Back* is a sobering look at this world. The average girl now joins social media before she turns thirteen. Before then, parents may innocently share information or images from her life that she didn't have a say in. Girls are likely cognizant of the fact that ostensibly private photos may eventually find a more public audience.[8] As Leah Plunkett of Harvard Law School and author of another book about parenting and the internet points out, there are consequences "if girls are raised to please the audience of a parent's camera and become aware that those pictures and videos are going to a larger audience."[9] The implicit message is this: Your worth is tied to satisfying others' needs.

THE PERFECTIONISM-FAILURE PARADOX

Leaders are not immune to this pressure to appear perfect. They often feel compelled to project an image of infallibility, fearing that any sign of imperfection will be perceived as weakness. The relentless pursuit of flawlessness leads to exhaustion and disengagement. Many of our survey respondents reported that they are negatively impacted by perfectionism. One woman shared that her fear of failure held her back and kept her from using her voice in meetings "for fear of being wrong or not being perceived as intelligent."[10]

This is an example of paralysis failure, in which perfectionism becomes so intense and so ingrained that it stops you from speaking up or taking action. And for many women, this fear of failure is reinforced by systemic biases that reward compliance over risk-taking, resulting in missed opportunities for advancement and personal growth. Perfectionists hesitate to apply for promotions or new opportunities unless they meet 100 percent of the qualifications (compared with men, who apply at 60 percent).[11] Women are also hesitant to self-promote, with only 13 percent saying they actively promote their success to their leaders and peers.[12] And perfectionists often delay projects because they fear they won't be done "right," but in reality, this avoidance increases stress and erodes confidence.

Burnout, procrastination, and fear are all ways that perfectionism not only fails to protect us from failure but also exacerbates tendencies that can lead to failure—or at least stifle growth and innovation.

LET GO OF PERFECTIONISM (OR MAKE IT WORK FOR YOU!)

Sarah Chen-Spellings, a venture capitalist and entrepreneur, knows firsthand how perfectionism can stifle ambition. Early in her career, she dreamed of launching her own startup but hesitated for years, convinced that she needed the perfect business plan, the perfect timing, and the perfect skill set before taking the leap.[13]

As a woman in the male-dominated world of venture capital, Sarah had absorbed the unspoken rule: Women must be twice as good to be taken seriously. Every detail had to be flawless. But perfectionism became her biggest barrier; it kept her stuck in the planning phase while male peers took risks, failed, and improved with each iteration.

Her breakthrough came when a mentor told her, "If you wait for perfection, you'll never start." With that in mind, she took the plunge, launching her first company before she felt fully ready. It wasn't perfect, and she made mistakes. But those missteps taught her invaluable lessons, and within a few years, she had successfully scaled and exited her business. Today, as cofounder of Beyond The Billion, she helps female founders secure venture funding, encouraging them to take bold risks rather than waiting for impossible perfection.

Her lesson? Action beats perfection. The key to success isn't getting everything right; it's moving forward, learning from failure, and iterating along the way.

CHOOSE EXCELLENCE OVER PERFECTION

The shift from "I must be flawless or I'm worthless" to "I want to do excellent work" often happens through a defining moment of letting go.

For Fiona, that moment came after selling her first company. Years of being underestimated as a young professional in an industry dominated by much older peers had fostered an exhausting need to be perfect to prove herself. Letting go of that impossible standard while keeping her drive for excellence was what finally allowed her to express her entrepreneurial ambition with a joyful "good enough" attitude.

The solution isn't abandoning high standards altogether. It's learning to tell the difference between striving for excellence and chasing impossible perfection. Keep the drive for continuous improvement and resilience. Let go of the rest.

DEB

I shifted away from perfectionism in college, when I started performing improvisational comedy. I learned that getting it exactly right was anathema to one of the tenets of improv: There are no wrong answers. Performing with a troupe of fellow improvisers who were equally committed to staying in the moment, listening to each other, building on each other's ideas, and running bold experiments helped me shed my perfectionistic mindsets and behaviors. And to this day, I consider my seven years performing improv—with its hilarious successes and heartbreaking bombs—the best training I've had for work and life.

And sometimes in life, the trials of your youth surface again as you try to help your children navigate similar circumstances. All of my experience with perfectionism—from my pursuit of academic excellence in high school to learning to let go through improv—came back to me as I watched my daughter, Sophie, struggle. Sophie had been a perfectionist her entire life—an A+ student and high school valedictorian. But by the time she got to Duke University, the pressure she put on herself had become overwhelming.

In her second semester, she was on track for an A– in a psychology course when the professor gave students a choice: Take the final exam and write an essay to improve their grade, or accept their current grade as final. Sophie realized this was a defining moment. If she took the A–, she would no longer have a perfect GPA—freeing herself from the impossible standard she had been chasing. She let go, chose balance over perfection, and later reflected, "My well-being is worth more than a grade." I was and am so proud of Sophie for recognizing that she was in charge of rewriting her success story.

Key Takeaways

- **Distinguish adaptive from maladaptive perfectionism:** High standards fuel success; fear-based perfectionism creates paralysis.
- **Choose progress over perfection:** Small, consistent actions toward your goals matter more than flawless execution.
- **Good enough is good enough:** Let something be good enough instead of perfect. See how it frees you to move forward.

CHAPTER 4

The Feedback Problem— Why Women Don't Get What They Need

When American chef Carla Hall was a contestant on Season 5 of the Emmy-winning TV show *Top Chef*, she quickly became a fan favorite because of her quirky personality and positive outlook. But standing in the spotlight and receiving feedback from her fellow contestants and the judges were part of her personal and professional growth trajectory.

In her first season of *Top Chef*, Carla's overt and covert feedback centered on the following two messages: You are too old to be here, and you are a caterer, not a chef. Carla's response was to prove them wrong. As a marathoner, she was physically so strong that she was "literally able to run circles around the younger people at age forty-two." But despite her mental, emotional, and physical fortitude, the feedback she got about her cooking often stung.

This wasn't new for Carla. When she was younger, she was very sensitive to feedback and focused a lot of energy on being liked. Words of affirmation were her love language, so criticism was very hard for her. As she matured, she learned that hearing and accepting (or rejecting) feedback was crucial for her success.

During Season 5 and then again during Season 8's *Top Chef: All Stars*, Carla grew to become comfortable with the uncomfortable. When someone said something she found hard to hear, she learned to physically stand in the feedback, feeling it in her body and trying not to push it away.

In 2024, Carla was bestowed the Grande Dame Award from Les Dames d'Escoffier, an honor awarded biennially to an exceptional woman in recognition of extraordinary contributions within the fields of food, beverage, and hospitality.

As a Black woman in the culinary and media worlds, feedback impacted the food she did and didn't want to make. Carla felt stuck between being the person people expected her to be and the person she actually is. During Season 8 of *Top Chef: All Stars*, Carla and her competitors were challenged to make a high protein dish for athletes. She made a groundnut soup but was worried that she'd be seen as "the Black girl who wants to do an African stew." As Carla remarked, "Nobody outside of my culture could understand the significance of this stew." Nevertheless, the feedback she received was powerful. "That soup could be perceived as very homey," award-winning Chef Tony Mantuano remarked, "but the steps you took really elevated it. It was a real surprise for me." Carla won the challenge, representing her family roots and Southern/African culinary heritage. The feedback helped her lean into her authentic self—and she's never turned away from that. Then, after proving her breadth of culinary talent as a finalist in both seasons of *Top Chef*, she did choose to become a comfort food chef, with soul food at its core. She cites the feedback she got from her "future fans" as giving her the confidence to lean into her true self. When she opened Carla Hall's Southern Kitchen, her restaurant in Brooklyn, New York, she was owning her history, her culture, and herself.

Carla believes that the people around her are messengers bringing her either lessons or blessings. She is committed to standing in the feedback she gets, letting it ground her, moving on, and getting to the other side. And now she says, "I love feedback because it's how I grow. And I love this version of me."

THE STATE OF FEEDBACK AND SUPPORT FOR WOMEN

Feedback is a critical element in the failure equation. In the best circumstances—in an environment where mistakes and failing are normalized and where there is a high degree of psychological safety and support for risk-taking—failure becomes its own kind of feedback. And while that feedback is not necessarily easy to swallow, it can nonetheless lead to learning and growth. But not all women get the kind of feedback they can readily translate into growth and learning. One of our survey respondents give a glimpse of the problem, explaining what was holding her back was being "criticized without any suggestions to make it better and then having that criticism used against me in a performance review regardless of whether I've since improved."[1]

WOMEN GET LOW-QUALITY FEEDBACK

Feedback for women is often subjective and vague, focused more on personality and "red herring" topics as opposed to leadership skills and business outcomes. While men are given concrete advice on leadership and strategic thinking, women's reviews often focus on personality traits, like being collaborative or approachable. This lack of actionable feedback makes it harder for women to develop confidence in their leadership abilities. Vague feedback often leaves women experiencing identity failure, questioning not just their performance but also their fundamental competence.

Performance reviews are a perfect example. Done correctly, they provide an ideal opportunity to tell a promising employee what they are doing well, what they can do better, and how they can do better. But research published in the *Harvard Business Review* finds women are consistently shortchanged by these reviews. While men receive feedback that is constructive and objective, women are 1.4 times more likely to get feedback that is critical and subjective. As a case in point, the research quotes one review of a woman who was criticized for her tendency "to shrink when she's around others, especially clients." This same challenge in a man was given a positive spin: "Jim needs to develop his natural ability to work with people."[2]

Another study of performance reviews at a large tech company found that even when feedback for women is positive, it tends to be vague, not specifying which actions or business outcomes were involved:

- 57 percent of reviews for women contained vague praise, compared to 43 percent for men.
- Men received developmental feedback directly linked to business outcomes 60 percent of the time, women only 40 percent.
- Criticisms for being "too aggressive" appeared in 76 percent of women's reviews and only 24 percent of men's.[3]

Without clear, actionable feedback tied to business outcomes, women can't build the targeted skills needed for advancement. This creates a cycle in which unclear expectations lead to uncertain performance, which gets misinterpreted as lack of confidence.

Criticisms of how a woman's voice sounds—her vocal tone is too high or too low, too loud or too soft, too aggressive or not authoritative enough—are just one instance of a long laundry list of frequent critiques of personal or intrinsic characteristics that are not changeable—and that also have nothing to do with job performance! In other words, they are the polar opposite of constructive criticism. Researchers Amy Diehl, Leanne M. Dzubinski, and Amber L. Stephenson say all of these surface-level criticisms—which include race, age, parental status, attractiveness, and physical ability—are essentially red herrings. They are "never quite right" criticisms telling women they are "too" this or "not enough" that.[4]

This "damned if you do, doomed if you don't" set of impossible standards for women has been described as the double-bind dilemma.[5] One particularly vexing catch-22 women face is that the more they are assessed as competent, the less they are seen as likable. The reverse holds true as well: A likable woman is seen as less competent. There is no zero-sum competition between these two qualities for men. They can be seen as likable or competent or both; one does not count against the other. Women face impossible choices that men don't encounter. Understanding this helps explain why strategic women might appear less confident: They're navigating constraints that don't exist for their male colleagues.

"When people don't receive [quality] feedback, they are less likely to know their worth in negotiations," write Catherine Tinsley, faculty director of the Women's Leadership Institute at Georgetown University, and Robin Ely, professor of business administration at Harvard Business School. "Moreover, people who receive little feedback are ill-equipped to assess their strengths, shore up their weaknesses, and judge their prospects for success and are therefore less able to build the confidence they need to proactively seek promotions or make risky decisions."[6]

Performance reviews often drift from judging performance to critiquing personality, and women of color are hit the hardest. In one Stanford study of 177 tech industry reviews, nearly 88 percent of the feedback for women included negative personality critiques, compared with just 2 percent for men. Words like *abrasive, bossy, strident,* and *emotional* popped up 17 times to describe 13 different women and almost never to describe men.[7]

Across 23,000 reviews, women were 22 percent more likely to get tagged with personality terms like *abrasive, difficult,* or *friendly,* while men were far more likely to be praised with labels tied to intellect, like *intelligent* or *gifted.* White and Asian men, in particular, were more than twice as likely to be called intelligent compared with Black or Hispanic/Latino peers.[8]

For women of color, the bias cuts especially deep. They are consistently downgraded by managers, even when their self-evaluations are strong. The problem is not ability but the lens through which their performance is judged.[9]

Although feedback is so often unproductive for women, it is essential for professional growth and development. "I've found that male or female, the executives who are the most successful are the best at taking feedback, and they seek it their whole lives," says executive coach Suzanne Bates. She encourages women to proactively seek out feedback from their network in order to develop that feedback "muscle."[10]

In her workshops on giving and receiving feedback, Deb takes it one step further by encouraging women to advocate for exactly the kind of feedback they need to advance their careers. This includes requesting feedback that is focused on leadership competencies and business outcomes. And, as Deb reminds her colleagues, you may have to ask multiple times to get what you need.

Key Takeaways

- **Demand quality feedback:** Insist on specific, actionable guidance tied to business outcomes rather than vague personality critiques. Ask, "What specific behaviors would improve my performance or outcomes?" to get clear next steps.

- **Build your feedback network:** Cultivate relationships with mentors, sponsors, and peers who can provide different types of support and perspective.

- **Develop a feedback routine:** Regularly and repeatedly ask for honest and helpful feedback from people who are committed to your growth and success. You may need to ask more than once to get what you need.

PART 2

Aim High—Rethinking Your Fear of Failure

Now that you understand why failure feels so threatening and how systemic barriers shape women's experiences with setbacks, it's time to shift from analysis to action. You can transform failure from an enemy into an ally by building the psychological tools and strategic frameworks that give you the confidence to aim high despite uncertainty.

This isn't about eliminating fear or avoiding setbacks. The most successful people don't fear failure less; they respond to it differently, with a set of evidence-based tools that help them take intelligent risks, navigate the inevitable challenges, and bounce back stronger when things don't go as planned.

CHAPTER 5

Transforming Your Relationship with Failure

At the age of twenty-two, Whitney Wolfe Herd joined a fledgling dating app called Tinder as cofounder and vice president of marketing. Her creative guerrilla tactics fueled Tinder's explosive growth on college campuses. But after only two years, she resigned amid tensions with other executives and filed a sexual harassment lawsuit. After leaving Tinder and confronting intense emotional backlash, Whitney described the experience in a *Vogue* interview as "horrible," reflecting a period of deep depression and trauma.[1]

The legal battle became what she later described as a "scarlet letter," making it difficult to hire employees or be taken seriously by potential partners as she explored new business ideas.[2] But she was undeterred.

"Start somewhere and go for it," she said, suggesting that a first step can be as simple as writing an idea "on a piece of paper and putting it on your bathroom mirror and staring at it for two weeks."[3] Her philosophy was clear: "I'd rather take a leap of faith and fall than stand on the edge forever."[4]

When an investor approached her about launching Bumble—a dating app where women message first—she pushed through early skepticism. "You will always have people telling you it's stupid and you just need to stay on track," she told ForbesWomen.[5] In February 2021, Bumble's IPO made her the youngest self-made female billionaire at 31.

But success brought new fears—even during the IPO celebration, where "her success at Bumble had cast her as the Kill Bill of the tech world: a yellow-clad woman seeking vengeance after men tried to bury her."[6]

With success, Whitney's fear shifted to the terror of losing what she'd built. "I was so scared . . . that I wouldn't make the right choices . . . I didn't want someone to judge me," she confessed to *Fortune*.[7] She stepped down as CEO in 2023. "I was so swept up in this external validation that I would not follow my instincts on things, and it degraded me. It took everything out of me."[8]

When Whitney returned as CEO in March 2025, something fundamental had shifted. "Now I'm back with this fresh mindset—my ego was stripped away. It's gone. I don't care if people like me. . . . I've broken up with not enjoying my life."[9]

Whitney's decade-long journey illustrates a crucial truth: Transforming your relationship with failure isn't magic, and it isn't reserved for a lucky few.

LISTENING TO AND LEARNING FROM YOUR FEAR PATTERNS

The fear of failure often influences daily decisions in ways you may not recognize. It shows up in small everyday choices that seem perfectly reasonable at the time:

- **The Overpreparation Trap:** You spend twice as long preparing for meetings or presentations as necessary, believing perfect preparation will eliminate the possibility of failure.

- **The Safe-Choice Default:** When faced with two options—one safe, one challenging—you automatically choose safety, even when the challenging option aligns better with your goals.

- **The Comparison Spiral:** You constantly measure your progress against others' highlight reels, interpreting normal learning curves as evidence you're not cut out for bigger challenges.

- **The Perfectionist Paralysis:** You delay launching, applying, or sharing your work because it doesn't feel ready enough, missing opportunities while waiting for impossible certainty.

- **The Story Amplification:** You create elaborate narratives about what others will think if you fail, often imagining reactions far more severe than reality would deliver.

We each have our own way of fear raising its ugly head and taking over. Fiona has a bias for action and is very entrepreneurial. And so she is surprised each time fear causes her to choose safety on work decisions that are very personal to her and feel tied up in her identity. For example, when she fundraises for her nonprofit, the WILD Network, that supports leaders who are tackling issues like access to clean water or helping children living in poverty, the stakes are so high that she feels she's putting a lot on the line each time she makes an ask, which can cause her to be hesitant. And it's clear to her that this tendency is holding back her women's leadership network from serving the greatest number of people with the greatest impact.

Deb wrestles with catastrophizing, anticipating the worst possible outcome. Ever since she was a child, Deb was told that she was "always waiting for the other shoe to drop." Now in her fifties, she has come to learn that she is resourceful enough to handle what comes her way, but the vestiges of catastrophizing are never completely wiped away.

So, what are your fear patterns, and what are they really telling you? If you can understand the pattern you frequently find yourself in, that can help you catch it in action. Here are some common behavioral patterns associated with the fear of failure; which of these patterns do you recognize in yourself?

- **Concrete Failure Response:** Interpreting specific setbacks as evidence of general inadequacy with thoughts like "I'm not good enough" or "I hit every metric but the one that mattered."

- **Paralysis Failure Response:** Using caution as an excuse to avoid meaningful risks; you may say to yourself, "Better safe than sorry" or "I became so good at avoiding failure that I also avoided success."

- **Identity Failure Response:** Conflating temporary roles or phases with permanent identity, which may feel like "I've lost myself completely" or "I don't like who I've had to become."

- **Circumstantial Failure Response:** Attributing setbacks to forces beyond your control; your thoughts may get stuck on the feeling that "everything bad happens to me."

- **Perceived Failure Response:** Assuming others judge your choices more harshly than they actually do, with "everyone thinks I'm a quitter" playing on repeat in your head.

There's no wrong response here. You're just gathering information about how your mind works so you can handle these situations more skillfully. Your patterns aren't permanent; they're just your starting point for transformation. And while your first instinct may reveal your current relationship with failure, the good news is it's within your control to change it.

LISTENING TO YOUR INTERNAL DATA

Beyond recognizing our fear patterns, we need to understand what gets in the way of trusting our own knowledge and experience. Too often, we discount our instincts in favor of external validation or corporate playbooks that weren't designed with us in mind. This is particularly critical for women of color, who face unique pressures to conform to templates of success built on what has historically worked for others.

FROM CONTRIBUTOR STEPHANIE LEBLANC-GODFREY
THE DATA OF YOU

The counterweight to all of the shoulds and assumptions and biases that come at us from the outside is the truth we hold onto on the inside—what I call the data of you. These are the lessons your own intuition, knowledge, and lived experience have taught you about your skills and passions, what you truly value, and what works for you.

You know these things in your bones, in an almost bodily way. But it's so easy to forget that data or discount it. You're operating in a corporate environment where the model of success is a template built on what has historically worked for other people—namely, frequently, white men. You're highly conscious of what all of the other people around you, of all races and genders, are doing to get ahead. It's easy to lose touch with your own path, the playbook that you know works for you. It's a difficult but worthy exercise to make a conscious effort to center your needs and your values in creating the life you want.

Here I want to make a full-throated case for therapy as useful skill-building work essential to both personal and professional self development. In my experience, therapy is building the vocabulary and understanding of how and why you veer away from the data of you and stop listening to yourself.

Personally, at some point, I recognized that I had internalized the fact that my parents were always in survival mode. When they accomplished something, they just moved on to the next thing. My husband pointed out that I never pause to acknowledge what I've accomplished. It's true, and I internalized that at a very early age. In third grade, I was practicing with SAT prep books. I'd learn ten new vocabulary words a week, write out the definition five times so I wouldn't forget, and then write a story at the end of the week to make sure I knew how to use them properly in a sentence. At the end of the week, I didn't get any recognition; I just got a new set of words. The message that sent me was keep going, keep grinding.

After considerable therapy, I came to the realization that I was skipping over a whole process that science now tells us is invaluable if we want to consolidate the gains we've made in our striving. Elite athletes know that they make their real gains in the rest and recovery stage after the stress of a hard workout. That's when you build muscle and endurance and resilience. It's the same in any endeavor. You need space to recognize what you've done and maybe reward yourself. And to rest. And to reflect on what you've accomplished and about the next step forward.

My parents didn't have the time, space, or luxury for those four Rs: recognition, reward, rest, and reflection. But I do. I don't have to be in survival mode 24/7. I have the freedom to be in thrive mode. But women of color like me have inherited that survival mode in our cultural DNA. We have to unpack that cultural inheritance and identify the tropes that no longer work for us. We have to learn to be able to celebrate and love the culture and bust the tropes.

FIONA

I've coached several women who accepted promotions that looked perfect on paper but felt wrong in their gut. One leader took a C-suite role managing a huge team, despite knowing she thrived in smaller, more strategic settings. Within eight months, she was exhausted, her team was floundering, and she questioned whether she was "executive material." The truth? She had been excellent at her previous role precisely because it aligned with her data. The new role didn't fail because of her abilities—it failed because she ignored what she already knew about how she works best. That misalignment cost her confidence, health, and two years of her career.

To start identifying your data, I ask my clients to reflect on two questions: When have you felt most energized and effective at work? What conditions allowed that? Then the counterpoint: When have you felt depleted or out of alignment, even while appearing successful to others? The patterns in your answers reveal your internal compass—what I call your data of you.

FLIP THE SCRIPT ON FAILURE

Some of the most successful women we interviewed had the healthiest relationships with failure—not because they avoided it but because they redefined what failure meant.

Our friend Ximena Sanchez, a communication executive, had to learn this lesson firsthand.[10] She stood up to a toxic and abusive boss, filing a formal complaint and taking the matter to the board of directors. Armed with her own story and those of other women who had suffered similar abuse, she was confident the board would take action.

They didn't.

It felt like the ground had been pulled from under her. She had risked everything to do the right thing, and it seemed like nothing had changed. The months that followed were filled with doubt, frustration, and the painful process of rebuilding.

But when she looked back, she realized she hadn't failed. She had been tested. And she had remained true to herself and her values. That was the success within the failure.

The experience left her more determined than ever to err on the side of taking big chances and going for it rather than accepting the failure of not trying. She briefly considered a safe landing spot, but it didn't feel right. She set out to write a book and then to start a new business in the middle of the pandemic. In neither case were the stakes as high as they had been in her previous situation. If the book or the business flopped, no one was going to care as much as her.

She told herself, "Get over yourself. Just try. If in two years the worst thing I have to say to someone is that I tried and it didn't work out, then I'll pivot to the next thing."

SHIFT YOUR RESPONSE FROM THREAT TO OPPORTUNITY

Working with professionals who've struggled with failure, we've noticed similar mental traps show up repeatedly. You know that voice in your head after something goes wrong? The one that immediately jumps to "I'm not cut out for this"? We've been there too.

But what we've learned is that the women who bounce back fastest aren't the ones who avoid those thoughts entirely. They're the ones who've learned to notice them and consciously shift to another track. These shifts don't happen overnight. We're talking about rewiring patterns you've probably had for years. But once you start catching these old mindsets in action, you can begin to shift to a different response.

DEB

Shifting from Verdict to Information

I remember the moment my coaching business nearly collapsed during the 2008 financial crisis. My first thought? "I'm clearly not cut out to run a business." It felt like a final verdict on my entrepreneurial abilities. But then something shifted. Instead of asking, "Why am I failing?" I started asking, "How can I grow from this situation?" Since I needed to earn money, I took a life-changing opportunity to teach Executive Communications at the Beijing International MBA Program at Peking University. In addition to providing a solid paycheck, this assignment gave me invaluable insights into cross-cultural communication and nonnative English speakers. I turned those new insights into a book, a live instructor-led program, and an online course. And what's more is that when Wharton was looking for new educators to teach communication skills to their MBA students, experience working with nonnative English speakers was a primary requirement. I got the job, which opened up further professional doors for me down the road, all because my business "failed" for a short period of time in the US economy.

The shift from verdict to information isn't just positive thinking. It's neurological rewriting. When your brain categorizes failure as an event, it triggers threat responses that impair clear thinking. When you see failure as information, it activates learning centers, enhancing problem-solving abilities.[11]

Here's what this sounds like in practice:

- Instead of "I bombed that presentation," try "I learned that I need to practice my opening more."
- Instead of "I'm terrible at negotiations," consider "I need different strategies for high-stakes conversations."

In the classes she teaches at Harvard Business School, Professor Frances Frei has found that showing a female faculty member a video of herself struggling while doing a video presentation is, to put it mildly, counterproductive. She will be distracted by self-consciousness about how she is performing, which is difficult to shrug off after years of knowing how women are endlessly scrutinized. (Conversely, watching a similar video is highly effective in helping men improve their skills.)

What does work for women is simply to sit down with the student for a one-on-one session to coach her through ways to improve. It's not different feedback; it's a different strategy.[12]

The people who bounce back fastest have mastered this mental and practical pivot. They don't skip the disappointment. They just don't let it become their identity.

FIONA
Shifting from Hypersensitive to Calibrated

I used to treat every piece of critical feedback like a five-alarm fire. A client's suggestion to adjust the agenda? Crisis. A speaker requesting a different time slot? Disaster. My internal alarm system was set so sensitively that routine business challenges felt like existential threats.

I learned this lesson the hard way when a longtime client sent me an email that simply said, "Hi, Fiona, I need to discuss some concerns about next week's workshop. Can we talk tomorrow?" That was it. No details, no context, just "concerns."

My mind immediately went to the worst possible scenario. They were canceling. They questioned my competence. They were probably telling other clients about whatever I'd done wrong. I spent that entire night drafting defensive emails, rehearsing explanations for mistakes I wasn't even sure I'd made. By morning, I'd convinced myself that my professional reputation was hanging by a thread.

The next day's phone call lasted exactly five minutes. The client's "concerns"? They needed to move the workshop start time from 9 a.m. to 10 a.m. because their CEO had a last-minute conflict. That was it. In fact, they spent most of the call praising my previous work and asking if I could recommend similar workshops for their other divisions.

I hung up feeling relief and also frustration at myself. I'd lost a night's sleep over a scheduling adjustment. But more importantly, I realized this wasn't the first time. Any email containing words like "concerns," "feedback," or "we need to talk" sent me into full panic mode, even when the actual conversation turned out to be routine business.

Now when I get those ambiguous emails, I ask myself, "What would I tell a friend if their client wanted to discuss logistics?" Usually, I'd say, "It's probably nothing major. Just call and find out." Learning to recalibrate means asking yourself, "Is this actually a crisis or just Tuesday?" Often, you'll realize you're treating routine challenges like catastrophes. And if you do receive a critique, treat the client feedback as useful data that's going to help you to retain that client and attract new customers!

Shifting from Hoping to Preparing

Many people approach potential failure like they approach turbulence on a plane: They close their eyes and hope for the best. But successful leaders create a flight plan for rough weather.

When Fiona co-led her first Next Chapter Accelerator Walking Retreat on the Camino de Santiago in Northern Spain during October, she knew there was the risk of rain. And if you've ever hiked in the rain, it can, well, dampen the experience! Even though the weather was outside of Fiona's control, they knew that a cold and wet day could detract from everyone's overall experience and reflect poorly on the reviews they would receive. So they made a contingency plan: They would bring rainy day snacks to enable their group to push through a rainy hike by eating lunch on the go. Then, once they reached the town where they were spending the night, the group could dry off and have a nice, large meal to make up for the quick lunch. They also increased the luggage allowance for each attendee to allow them to pack an extra set of hiking boots just in case the rain soaked their main pair. That way, Fiona, her colleague, and the group felt prepared for whatever Mother Nature might have in store.

Think about your last big presentation or project launch. Did you spend more time hoping nothing would go wrong or preparing for what you'd do if something did? Deb has delivered keynote speeches in no fewer than three blackouts! Not only did the PowerPoint not work, but neither did the toilets! And while she had very little control over the latter, she was prepared for the former and delivered her speeches without visual aids. Her ability to adapt on the spot added to her credibility as a speaker who could teach others to deal with setbacks as they arise.

When you have a specific plan for handling setbacks, challenges stop feeling catastrophic and start feeling manageable. Preparing for problems isn't pessimism. It's strategic thinking. You're not expecting to fail; you're expecting to be ready.

Shifting from Perfect Performance to Meaningful Progress

The traditional scorecard for success is pretty brutal: Did you avoid all mistakes? Did everything go according to plan? For most ambitious goals, the answer is usually no, which makes the whole endeavor feel like failure.

> **DEB**
>
> When my daughter, Sophie, and I wrote our first coauthored book, *Overcoming Overthinking: 36 Ways to Tame Anxiety for Work, School, and Life*, in 2019, we hoped that the book would become a best seller—and maybe even win some awards. After all, who isn't wrestling with overthinking? Nevertheless, the book hasn't become a bestseller—or even a brisk seller—in the years since it's been published. However, we receive emails on a regular basis from readers around the world who have been touched by the book's compassionate messages—and

first-person stories—about managing often-debilitating anxiety. Hearing from readers who have shared how the strategies in the book have helped them means more to us than big awards or public accolades. We know that we're touching people's lives in a meaningful way—and that is success.

So, what if, like Deb and Sophie, you kept score differently? What if instead of asking if you messed up, you asked the following:

- How many new things did I try?
- What skills did I develop?
- How quickly did I recover from setbacks?
- What value did I create, even if the execution wasn't perfect?
- Who was positively impacted?

Professionals who track these learning metrics alongside traditional outcomes don't just feel better about their progress. They actually advance faster in their careers and report higher job satisfaction. It turns out that celebrating courage and growth isn't just nice; it's strategic.

Shifting from Judgment Assumption to Reality Testing

Here's something counterintuitive: Sharing your failures openly doesn't damage your reputation. It enhances it. We know this goes against every instinct you have about professional image management. Most of us avoid talking about our setbacks because we assume others will judge us harshly. However, vulnerability and authentic sharing actually increase trust and leadership effectiveness among colleagues.[13] The thing you think will make people lose respect for you, done right, actually makes them respect you more. This doesn't mean oversharing every struggle in every meeting. It means being honest about the learning process and giving others permission to be human too.

PRACTICE MAKES PROGRESS (NOT PERFECTION)

Once you've identified your fear patterns and understood the mental shifts that help you move past the fear of failure, it's time to practice. Here are ways to make these new responses automatic.

Practicing the Shift from Verdict to Information

Remember Deb's story about reframing her business crises? You can learn to do the same thing.

When something goes wrong this week, catch yourself before the verdict (the thought of "I'm not cut out for this") and ask one simple question: "What information does this give me?" When projects don't go as planned, ask yourself, "What can I learn from this?" Then take it a step further and identify one hypothesis you can test today. For example, "If I do X, I predict Y will happen based on what I learned yesterday," and stay open to what happens. The key is shifting your mindset from "I was wrong" to "I was experimenting and now I have new information."

Fiona keeps a learning log. When she's experimenting with a new line of business or innovation or when things don't always go as planned, she writes down these specific things: "Start, stop, continue, and why." Changing the question from "why did I fail?" to "what did I learn?" completely shifts how she feels about setbacks and helps her and her colleagues process the learning faster.

You'll know it's working when you catch yourself getting curious about failure instead of just feeling defeated by it. That moment when your brain automatically asks, "What can I learn?" before it finishes the thought, "I'm terrible at this" is real progress!

Practicing the Shift from Hypersensitive to Calibrated

Remember Fiona's sleepless night over that "concerns" email that turned out to be a scheduling change? You may have your own version of this kind of story.

When you feel the familiar panic rising—whether it's from ambiguous feedback or a challenge, question, or unexpected request—try Fiona's technique yourself and ask yourself, "What would I tell my best friend if this happened to her?" Usually, you'd say something like, "It's probably nothing major. Just call and find out."

Start small with low-stakes situations. The next time you get a vague email or ambiguous feedback, notice your first reaction; then, consciously choose to respond as if it's routine business. Practice the pause before the panic. You'll notice the difference when "we need to talk" stops sending you into a spiral and starts feeling like normal communication.

Practicing the Shift from Hoping to Preparing

Think about Fiona's hiking example of bringing extra snacks and boots in case of a rainy day. The same thinking works for work situations.

For your next important presentation, meeting, or project, spend equal time planning what you'll do if things go perfectly and what you'll do if they don't. Deb advises her clients to practice by taking a micro-risk with a backup plan, like sharing your opinion in a meeting and having a response planned if someone challenges you.

After each situation, compare what actually occurred versus what you feared would happen. Make sure to focus on the facts rather than an emotion-driven story you make up about what happened and the meaning you're infusing into it. Consider recruiting an accountability partner who models and encourages thoughtful, calculated risk-taking.

This reality testing helps recalibrate your risk assessment over time. You'll now feel prepared instead of anxious and have genuine confidence going into uncertain situations because you know you can handle whatever comes up.

Practicing the Shift from Perfect Performance to Meaningful Progress

Traditional scorecards in business focus only on flawless execution. But what if you measured different things?

For example, Deb encourages her clients to keep a courage journal—not for recording successes but for documenting the moments they chose growth over comfort. They write down every time they spoke up when they would have stayed quiet or tried something new when they would have played it safe. It's amazing how much progress you can see when you're measuring the right things.

Celebrate completion over perfection. The next time you finish something (a project, a difficult conversation, or a presentation), take a moment to acknowledge that you did it, regardless of how it went. Finished beats perfect every single time.

Something shifts when you start feeling proud of your willingness to try new things, not just your ability to execute them flawlessly, when "I learned something" starts feeling as satisfying as "I nailed it."

Practicing the Shift from Judgment Assumption to Reality Testing

Most of us fear that we'll lose others' trust in our abilities if we share our experiences with failure. However, in Fiona's FailLab sessions, sharing struggles actually increased trust.

To move away from assuming we're being judged, start with small acts of authenticity. Choose your top five values, and make one decision today that aligns with at least two of them. In a low-risk environment, share a personal story, a perspective you have, or a belief you hold. Notice people's actual responses versus what you expected.

Identify five people in your life who appreciate, celebrate, and cherish you as you are. Keep them in mind as you make choices throughout the day. When you catch yourself assuming what others are thinking, challenge yourself to gather actual evidence.

Try the reality test question: "If my best friend made this same mistake, would I think less of her?" The answer is almost always no, and other people are probably extending to you the same grace that you'd give to a friend.

The time will come when you start sharing challenges and lessons learned more naturally and when you stop crafting elaborate stories about what others must be thinking. You'll likely realize that most people are too busy worrying about their own performance to judge yours harshly.

YOUR FIVE-MINUTE DAILY CHECK-IN

Each evening, spend five minutes thinking about one thing that didn't go as planned that day. Then try reframing it using whichever shift feels most useful. Pay attention to how differently you feel about the experience when you do this.

Keep practicing these approaches. Just five minutes a day starts rewiring how your brain works. When you change how you think about failure, everything else shifts too—how you handle challenges and make decisions, even what opportunities you're willing to pursue.

Think about Whitney Wolfe Herd's journey over ten years. That's what we're going for—not some magical overnight change but steady progress toward handling failure in a completely different way, in which setbacks become useful information and your worst moments end up teaching you the most valuable lessons.

Practice these strategies regularly to help them become habits.

Key Takeaways

- **Use failure as feedback, not judgment:** Instead of "Why did I fail?" ask, "What can I learn from this?" This shifts your brain from judgment mode to learning mode.

- **Dig into your failures:** When setbacks occur, acknowledge the failure, learn from the failure, and mine it for useful data for the next time.

- **Transform your response:** Make the shifts from overpreparation to strategic preparation, from perfectionist paralysis to accepting good enough, and from catastrophizing to realistic planning. Catching these automatic responses is the first step to choosing different reactions.

- **Be patient with yourself:** Transformation is possible at any stage of your career. Your relationship with failure can evolve over a year, a decade, or your entire career.

CHAPTER 6

How Entrepreneurs Turn Setbacks into Strategic Advantages

After her hundredth investor rejection, nineteen-year-old Melanie Perkins faced a choice: give up on her vision or find another way forward.[1]

Melanie had identified a clear problem while teaching design software to classmates at the University of Western Australia: students who spent weeks just figuring out where the buttons were. Most design programs were unnecessarily complex and intimidating for everyday users, but investors didn't see software complexity as a billion-dollar opportunity.

Rather than taking each no personally, Melanie treated the rejections as data. A transformative insight emerged from analyzing the pattern: "One of the most important things that we learned was that to convince investors of our idea, they had to be convinced that the problem existed and that the problem affected a lot of people," Melanie reflected.[2] This led her to completely restructure her pitch to lead with the emotional frustration before presenting any features.

Instead of continuing to chase investors for her grand vision, Melanie made a strategic retreat. With her boyfriend Cliff Obrecht, she created Fusion Books, an online yearbook design business that would prove the market existed. "My mum's living room became my office, and my boyfriend became my business partner, and we started enabling schools to create their yearbooks really, really simply," Melanie explained. This smaller venture let them test their core assumptions about simple design tools while building a track record that might eventually convince investors.

This scaled-down experiment revealed crucial blind spots. Initially, Melanie and Cliff assumed schools would immediately embrace online collaboration and simple design tools. Instead, user testing revealed that many schools were hesitant to move away from traditional yearbook processes and needed significant education about the benefits. "We spent months building features we thought schools wanted, only to find they were confused by too many options," Melanie recalled.

When they eventually secured funding and developed Canva years later, they carried forward this commitment to putting their product in front of customers, learning about weaknesses and addressing them systematically.[3]

Through this process, Melanie learned what research confirms: 90 percent of startups fail not because they can't build their product but because they build something nobody wants.[4]

After years of systematic experimentation and customer feedback, Melanie's approach led to Canva's extraordinary success. By August 2025, the company was valued at over $42 billion, with 240 million active users worldwide.[5]

Melanie's story shows how taking a disciplined entrepreneurial approach prevents failure. But what if you've already experienced a spectacular setback? Julie Wainwright's journey demonstrates that entrepreneurial principles work even after the most public failures.

In the late 1990s, Pets.com had everything: a quirky sock puppet mascot, the tagline "Because pets can't drive," backing from Amazon and venture capitalists. With Julie at the helm as CEO, the company went public in 2000. But selling heavy bags of dog food at a loss while paying for shipping? The economics never worked. Less than nine months after its IPO, Pets.com collapsed.[6]

The collapse came to symbolize everything wrong with the dot-com bubble. The company's memorable mascot, which had made it instantly recognizable through expensive Super Bowl ads and marketing campaigns, now made its failure impossible to forget.[7]

It was mocked on late-night television and immortalized in business case studies. And Julie, one of the very few female technology executives at that level at the time, became the public face of that failure.

On the same day Julie laid off her team, her husband of more than a decade asked for a divorce. Then came years of rejection.[8]

A recruiter told Julie that her failure as CEO of Pets.com made her prospects bleak.[9] As Julie recalled, "What I didn't realize until later was that I was pretty unemployable in the tech world after that."[10] Friends disappeared. The industry that once celebrated her closed its doors. "I had to find my own inner core because the industry that had allowed me to have an exciting career and a good career had turned its back on me and said I was a failure," she recalls.[11]

In 2011, she founded The RealReal, an online marketplace for authenticated secondhand luxury goods. The idea for the startup came from her own experience trying to consign luxury items: Authentication was inconsistent, trust low, and the customer experience unprofessional.

This time, there were no splashy ads or lavish launch events. Julie started at her kitchen table, doing the work herself. She picked up items from sellers, studied authentication, and handled deliveries.

Julie didn't shy away from her past. In investor meetings and media interviews, she spoke openly about Pets.com—not defensively but as a source of hard-won wisdom.

In 2019, The RealReal went public—Julie's second IPO. This time, she'd build something profitable and meaningful.

Julie's story shows what's possible when you refuse to let failure define you. The Pets.com disaster became the foundation for The RealReal. As her story shows, your lowest moment doesn't determine your future. What you build next does.

FROM CRYSTAL BALL TO LABORATORY: HOW ENTREPRENEURSHIP EDUCATION CHANGED

For decades, business schools taught entrepreneurship through one approach: Plan everything in advance. Students spent months writing elaborate forty-page business plans with five-year financial projections, detailed market analyses, and competitive assessments. The idea was simple: If you could plan well enough, you could predict and control your business's future.

There was just one problem: It didn't work. Most startups failed not because entrepreneurs couldn't execute their plans but because their plans were based on untested assumptions about what customers actually wanted.

The breakthrough came when educators realized they were teaching entrepreneurship backward. Instead of starting with elaborate plans full of educated guesses, successful entrepreneurs were starting with small experiments designed to test their assumptions quickly and cheaply.

This shift changed everything. Today's entrepreneurship students still create business plans, but they approach them very differently. Instead of spending months perfecting a single comprehensive plan, they learn to create quick one-page summaries that capture their key assumptions. Then they get out of the classroom and test those assumptions with real customers. When they discover their assumptions are wrong (which happens frequently), they adjust their approach and test again.

The old model taught students to avoid failure through better planning. The new model teaches them to learn from failure through better experimentation. Instead of trying to predict what will work, they're trying to discover what works.

THE ONE-PAGE REVOLUTION

Alex Osterwalder and Yves Pigneur revolutionized how people think about business planning. The Swiss entrepreneur was frustrated with traditional business plans that took months to write and were usually wrong anyway. So he created the Business Model Canvas, a one-page visual tool that captures the founder's key assumptions about customers, value propositions, and revenue streams.

The genius of Osterwalder's approach is that it treats a business plan as a series of hypothesis to be tested, not a prediction to be followed. Users fill out the canvas with educated assumptions, then systematically test each assumption with real customers. When you learn something new, you update the canvas. It's business planning designed for learning, not just planning.

FIONA
PLANNING TO FAIL

Before WILD's first Global Leadership for Social Impact Forum, which quickly became known as the WILD Forum, I stared at the pathetic sales dashboard: $1,290 in ticket sales in five days. I sat there, morning coffee in hand, and felt perplexed.

Fifteen years earlier, this would have sent me into a spiral of self-doubt and paralysis. I would have been expressing fears to my husband and been distracted at dinnertime, ruminating on how I was ruining my professional reputation and gnashing my teeth at night. But by the time I launched the WILD Network, my global network for purpose-driven women, I had learned to approach new lines of business with the scientific approach of a startup founder.

Before launching the WILD Forum, I had done everything right, according to startup methodology. I mapped out my assumptions. Customer segments were professional, purpose-driven women seeking to become even stronger leaders in a safe environment, who also wanted to build their networks and find fresh inspiration from ideas and tools inside and outside of their industry. I conducted systematic customer interviews, asking questions like "When was the last time you attended formal leadership training?" and "What was the most helpful thing you learned, how did you apply it, and what has it changed for you?" and "What are one or two leadership challenges you've faced in the last month?" and everyone's favorite question, "If you could change one thing about your manager, what would it be?"

Armed with research showing strong and enthusiastic demand for more leadership development, I felt confident about committing to a date, hiring a conference manager, and putting a deposit down on a venue, even though the date was only two months away.

Then reality delivered its lesson.

I felt that familiar knot forming in my stomach. For a split second, my brain started down the old path: What if I've made a terrible mistake? What if I ruin the reputation I have built over twenty years as a successful serial innovator and everyone thinks I'm incompetent? But then I literally stopped myself midthought and said out loud, "Okay, this is just data." That moment felt revolutionary.

Instead of panicking like the old me, I went back to my research like a scientist hunting for a missing variable. I combed through my interview notes, looking for what I'd missed. The breakthrough came when I realized I hadn't asked, "Who pays for the leadership development you've received?" When I went back and asked the question of employees, the answer was always the employer, not the individual employee. Only independent consultants were paying out of pocket.

This insight sparked my next experiment. I stopped spending time on marketing to individuals and sent thirty emails to executive teams whose employees were seeking leadership development. I repositioned the exact same conference as an investment in human capital to drive business results, with the added benefit of corporate team building for companies that sponsored tickets for a large group of their employees.

Six weeks later: $100,000 in sponsorships and ticket sales.

The same event that generated $1,290 in ticket sales in five days generated $100,000 when marketed to the economic buyer. I had been pitching to the wrong wallet. Professional women loved the idea of leadership development, but they weren't the economic buyers, and it was laborious for them to advocate to their bosses to access stipends for learning and development. Their companies held the training budgets and made the purchasing decisions. Nothing had changed about the conference except my understanding of who my real customer was.

I updated my Business Model Canvas accordingly. Customer segments evolved from individual professional women to HR departments and executive teams, and my value proposition added "team leadership capabilities that drive business results."

The difference between the mindset I had when I started my first company and the mindset I had with WILD wasn't the quality of my ideas. It was my relationship with expecting to get it right the first time—no gnashing of teeth at night, no panic attacks, no paralysis. I had moved from assuming that I could be perfect when experimenting with new ideas to holding onto the vision but being flexible about how I would get there.

Successful innovators learn how to fail fast and cheaply without damaging consequences, gather data and learn quickly, make smart pivots or adaptations, and keep moving toward something more successful.

They design a series of planned experiments, knowing they'll learn a little from each one. They expect most experiments to fail, but they fail forward, extracting valuable lessons that inform the next experiment. This lets them learn cheaply instead of betting everything on one test.

DEB

When COVID hit and I had to take my in-person workshops online, I started with my regular catalog of offerings to clients: presentation skills, difficult conversations, giving and receiving effective feedback, communicating with emotional intelligence, etc. I quickly learned two things:

- Employees weren't focused on developing new interpersonal skills; they were focused on surviving and coping.
- Clients no longer had the attention span for hours of learning when they were now on Zoom all day.

As a result of hearing no a lot, I started experimenting with what might resonate in these new times. I tested out new topics and new time frames. Ultimately, I pivoted to offering workshops on mental well-being at work and to delivering the content in half-hour bites. These bites added up over time: They became the basis for the book I wrote with my daughter, Sophie, *Go to Help: 31 Strategies to Offer, Ask for, and Accept Help*, as well as the curriculum for several self-paced courses addressing mental health in the workplace, a topic I care about deeply.

One of my proudest moments was when Sophie and I were invited to speak about mental well-being to a group of true American heroes, the United States Department of Homeland Security's first responders. My experimentation didn't just help my business and my clients survive; it also helped them thrive in ways I never anticipated.

TOOLS YOU CAN USE TO EMBRACE FAILURE LIKE A STARTUP

In persevering through failure, Melanie, Fiona, and Deb—consciously or not—all wielded tools entrepreneurs employ to turn failure into eventual success. Below is a list of tools that the most innovative companies use to turn failure into competitive advantage that may help you take a new look at failure:

- **Customer Discovery:** Before you build anything, talk to the people you think will use it. This sounds obvious, but most people skip this step because they're convinced they already know what customers want. This methodology, pioneered by entrepreneur and educator Steve Blank, revolutionized how startups approach product development by emphasizing learning from real customers rather than assumptions. Customer discovery is simply having conversations with potential users (without any sales pressure) before you invest time and money in solutions. The key is asking open-ended questions and really listening to the answers, even when they contradict what you hoped to hear.

- **The Build-Measure-Learn Cycle:** Instead of trying to create the perfect solution from day one, design something small, see how people react, and then improve it based on what you learn from the gap between your expectations and reality. Then reimagine the next version based on what you discovered. The goal isn't to avoid failure; it's to fail quickly and cheaply while you're still learning rather than expensively after you've committed everything.

- **Learning from Rejection:** When investors say no, that doesn't mean the idea is necessarily flawed. It may just mean there is a gap in information the investors have to evaluate your idea. Yes, rejection hurts, but you can take a little of the sting out by learning why the previous investor said no by revising your pitch to preemptively address the concern or question with other potential investors.

- **Thinking Like an Entrepreneur Inside Your Job:** Apply the same experimental mindset you might use for a new business to projects, initiatives, and challenges within your current organization. Instead of accepting "that's how we've always done it," ask what small experiment could test whether there's a better way. Treat resistance as information about what needs to change, not as a reason to give up.

- **Information Arbitrage:** As you get better at learning from failure, you leap ahead of others who repeat the same mistakes by systematically learning what works and what doesn't and building a database of insights that guides better decisions. People who master this approach don't just recover from setbacks faster; they use their failures as competitive intelligence—their secret weapon. Over time, this creates a significant advantage in decision-making, career progression, and business results.

- **Building Psychological Resilience:** Every successful entrepreneur has felt foolish, uncertain, and unqualified. The difference is they acted anyway, treating discomfort as data rather than a stop sign. As Fiona tells her Georgetown students, entrepreneurial courage means feeling the fear of being wrong and experimenting anyway.

DEB

My client Tali is a good example of the emotional work it can take to reposition failure as a learning opportunity. As the chief marketing officer of a leading tech company, she had built a reputation for driving innovative campaigns. But beneath her polished exterior, Tali grappled with an overwhelming fear of failure that affected both her professional performance and personal well-being.

Tali's breaking point came after a high-stakes product launch that didn't meet the company's ambitious sales targets. Though the campaign received positive feedback, the numbers were lower than expected. For Tali, it felt like a personal failure.

In her first coaching session, Tali shared her feelings of inadequacy. I asked, "What does failure mean to you?"

"It's an indication that I'm not good enough," Tali replied. "That I can't handle the responsibilities of my role."

I responded, "It sounds like you're equating failing at a task with being a failure as a person. Let's work on disentangling those two."

I introduced Tali to the concept of a growth mindset, explaining how failures are opportunities for learning rather than judgments of one's abilities. I invited Tali to practice viewing failure as feedback rather than a final verdict on her worth. I also helped Tali practice living with not knowing by exploring uncertain scenarios and developing strategies to navigate them with confidence.

This practice paid off. When a major merger required Tali to lead a complex integration of the two companies' personnel and processes, she approached it with her new mindset, acknowledging her fears without letting them paralyze her. This new skill set then helped her to communicate openly with her team and support them in viewing the changes caused by the merger as an opportunity to learn and adapt. That Tali's growth benefited both her and her team shows the compounding impact of learning to fail like an entrepreneur.

APPLYING ENTREPRENEURIAL THINKING TO CAREER CHANGES

Career changes work the same way as startups: They begin with untested assumptions about what you'll be good at, what you'll enjoy, and what the market values.

Instead of making major career pivots like quitting to go back to school or taking a new job in a different field based on assumptions, you can test your hypotheses through smaller experiments that give you real data about whether a career change makes sense before you commit to expensive, high-stakes decisions. Freelance in the area you're considering.

Take on a project that uses the skills you want to develop. Shadow someone whose job interests you. Want to try academia? Start with guest lecturing or an adjunct position to get a real taste of curriculum planning, classroom management, and department politics.

Fiona teaches this philosophy of designing small job-change experiments before making major moves in her Next Chapter Accelerator program. Working with mature, successful professional women who are considering their next career phase, she's learned that the fear around major changes is often well-founded. When you've worked hard to get to where you are, there are real financial, reputational, and opportunity risks in transitioning from an executive job to consulting, a portfolio career, or launching a venture. By replacing expensive, high-stakes decisions with smaller learning cycles, you'll gain information that helps you figure out what actually works for you.

Lee Ann, one of Fiona's coaching clients, spent twenty years as a tenured university professor before making a bold career shift to the nonprofit sector, where she served as an executive director of three organizations. Even with this impressive track record, she found herself ready for yet another reinvention.

Lee Ann recognized a common thread through everything she'd done: advancing women's empowerment by dismantling barriers to their wellbeing. This through line felt significant, yet she still lacked the clarity, knowledge, and confidence to pursue an entrepreneurial idea that had been quietly percolating in her mind for years. The breakthrough came during Fiona's walking retreat. "We explored the value of experimenting with low-risk opportunities," Lee Ann recalls. "This approach combined with the physical journey cleared my head and created space for fresh ideas, making a big undertaking feel more doable."

Instead of attempting to launch a full business right away, Lee Ann applied lean startup principles to her career transition. She designed small experiments to test her assumptions about coaching and women's leadership. Her first experiment was enrolling in a low-cost online program for aspiring leadership coaching—a minimal investment that would help her validate whether she enjoyed the work and had a natural aptitude for it.

Her second experiment came when she accepted an invitation to speak at a women's leadership conference, allowing her to test her coaching framework with a real audience and gather immediate feedback.

Each small experiment taught her something valuable and built her confidence to take the next step. Just like a startup testing product–market fit, Lee Ann was testing career–passion fit through real-world validation rather than endless planning. These systematic experiments led to the creation of Badass University LLC, equipping women with the tools, strategies, and mindsets they need to overcome challenges and step fully into their power.

Key Takeaways

- **Always be experimenting:** The entrepreneurial approach to failure isn't about being reckless. It's about being intentional, systematic, and strategic in how you design experiments, test your assumptions, and learn from the results. Expect most experiments to fail in some way, but know that each setback will teach you something valuable.

- **Make educated assumptions:** Before making major commitments, design cheap tests that can validate or invalidate your key assumptions. You're not trying to avoid failure; you're trying to fail in ways that move you forward.

- **Appreciate each step forward:** Each experiment should move you closer to your goal, even if it reveals what doesn't work.

CHAPTER 7

When the Fear of Failure Peaks—Navigating the Danger Zone of Doubt

Vera Wang's path to success illustrates a crucial mindset shift: Sometimes the fear of not trying becomes more dangerous than the fear of failing.

Vera worked as an assistant to legendary editor Polly Mellen and eventually became one of the youngest senior fashion editors.[1] In 1987, after seventeen years at *Vogue*, she was passed over for the editor-in-chief position she had worked toward, then left for Ralph Lauren.[2]

Then at age forty, Vera faced her defining moment. When she couldn't find a sophisticated modern wedding dress for her own 1989 wedding, she saw an opportunity. But this is where her mindset about failure became transformative. "I always sort of dreamed of being a fashion designer, and I thought, 'Well, if I don't try it now, I'm never going to be able to do it,'" she said.[3] Despite having no formal design training, she quit her stable job at Ralph Lauren and opened Vera Wang Bridal House in New York City.[4] Her willingness to risk failure paid off. Today, her brand generates more than $700 million in annual retail sales.[5]

Vera is honest about what choosing to try actually means: "There have been a million days where I said to myself, 'What was I thinking?' or 'Why did I do this?' But there have been way more days where I felt extremely lucky to be doing something that I love so much."[6] And that choice to try is powerful.

But what happens when you've already made that choice and find yourself deep in the challenge, questioning every decision? Sometimes the danger zone isn't about whether to start; it's about whether to keep going when doubt creeps in. How do we push forward when fear of failure feels overwhelming?

THE UNIVERSAL TRUTH ABOUT THE MIDDLE: IT'S F---ING MESSY!

Dr. Rosabeth Moss Kanter, a leading expert on organizational change and perseverance, has spent decades studying what separates those who persist through challenges from those who abandon their goals. Her research revealed a fundamental truth that every ambitious person must understand:[7]

> Welcome to the miserable middle of change. This is the time when Kanter's Law kicks in. Everything looks like a failure in the middle. Everyone loves inspiring beginnings and happy endings; it is just the middles that involve hard work.

This is what we call the danger zone of doubt: that moment when you're deep enough into something that quitting feels terrible, but not far enough to see the light at the end of the tunnel. Women are 40 percent more likely than men to abandon stretch goals during the first six months of pursuit.[8] Vera experienced this zone with her fashion line, just as countless women do when they're months into a challenging goal and everything seems to be falling apart. The danger zone is where dreams go to die, unless you understand how to navigate it.

You know you've hit the danger zone when your stomach drops every time you check email, wondering if today's the day everything falls apart. It's when you wake up at 3 a.m. replaying conversations, second-guessing decisions you felt confident about just weeks ago. It's when the voice in your head has turned into a full-blown critic blasting all the ways you're not qualified for what you're trying to do. It's the moment when scrolling though LinkedIn feels like psychological torture because everyone seems to have it figured out. It's when your partner asks, "How's it going?" and you're not sure whether you should lie, admit that you're questioning everything, or simply bite their head off.

That's what the danger zone actually feels like: not dramatic failure but slow burning doubt that makes you want to quit before anyone notices you might not succeed. But here's what the most successful people have learned to do in these moments: They've trained themselves to hear something different.

Carol Dweck, the researcher behind growth mindset, then was inspired by a school that didn't give failing grades. She saw something powerful. Instead of marking papers with an F, teachers wrote "Not Yet"[9]—six letters that completely change how you think about setbacks. Frances Frei collected five rejections from Harvard before becoming their first LGBTQ+ tenured professor.[10] She didn't hear "no" in those rejections. She heard "not now." When Dolly Chugh's second book didn't have the commercial success of her first, she told us that she didn't think, "I'm a failure." She thought, "It's not a bestseller . . . yet."

This is what the danger zone actually feels like when you know how to navigate it: not a dramatic failure but a temporary "not yet" moment that's preparing you for what comes next.

WHEN FEARS CONVERGE AND THEN SPIRAL

The danger zone gets especially brutal for women because suddenly, multiple fears hit you all at once. Think about Sarah, a client Fiona coaches. She was three months into launching a tech startup that's changing the way the energy sector does their hiring when she faced her first major client crisis. Suddenly, four different fears hit her all at once.

First, the visibility fear whispered that everyone was watching to see whether she'd succeed. This wasn't paranoia; it was pattern recognition. Research backs up what women already know: Our mistakes get noticed more and punished harder.[11]

Second, the judgment fear made this pressure worse. Sarah worried that if she failed, it would confirm the doubts of those who questioned her decision to leave corporate security. Third, the identity fear, which cuts deepest, suggested that if this venture didn't work, what did that say about who she really was? And finally, the opportunity fear haunted her with the possibility that failure here meant never getting another chance.

These fears not only converged, but they also started to spiral. Her story is an example of the fear spiral in action; you may recognize yourself in this pattern.

Maria, another client Fiona coaches, is a software engineer getting her MBA while working full-time. In her second semester, the workload intensified beyond what she anticipated. First, she became hypervigilant, scanning for signs of impending failure and interpreting normal academic challenges as crisis signals. A B+ on her first strategy assignment became evidence that she wasn't MBA material.

Next came defensive decision-making. Instead of pursuing the most challenging courses that would accelerate her growth, Maria began choosing safer options to minimize the risk of obvious failure. She dropped the advanced finance course she'd been excited about, telling herself she needed to be realistic.

Then came the exhaustion. Constant worry about failure consumed the mental resources she needed for actual performance . . . followed by self-sabotage. Overwhelmed by failure anxiety, Maria began considering dropping out entirely. "Maybe I'm just not cut out for this," she told her wife, even though her grades remained above average and her professors praised her practical insights.

The spiral becomes less dangerous when you recognize its early signals. The danger zone gives you warning signs, like storm clouds before bad weather. Here are the three biggest ones:

- **Catastrophic thinking takes over:** You find yourself imagining worst-case scenarios and treating them as likely outcomes. Your brain starts treating unlikely disasters like certainties.
- **Standards become impossible:** You start believing that anything less than flawless execution equals failure. The quality orientation that once served as a competitive advantage transforms into a prison of perfectionism. If you fall into a "compare and despair" trap, it can be especially brutal.
- **Analysis paralysis sets in:** You keep researching, planning, and preparing instead of taking action. The irony is cruel: The more you fear failure, the more you delay the actions that could prevent it.

WHAT HELPS YOU GET THROUGH THE DANGER ZONE

When you're experiencing the warning signs that you are entering the danger zone, having the right environment and support makes all the difference. Sometimes that support is within you; sometimes it's around you.

Your Personal Danger Zone Tool Kit

When you're in crisis mode and your brain is spinning, you don't need ten different strategies. You need the three that actually work when you're panicking.

- **Start with the "so what?" reality check:** This cuts through the noise faster than anything else. For each scary scenario your brain is cooking up, ask yourself, "Okay, so what would actually happen if this came true?" If this project doesn't work out, so what? You'd learn something valuable and try again smarter. If people judge you, so what? The people who matter will respect that you tried something hard.

- **Next, make your failure plan:** We know this sounds weird, but spend fifteen minutes writing down exactly what you'd do if things went sideways. Who would you call for advice? What would you learn from the experience? What would your next move be? Having a failure plan paradoxically reduces failure anxiety because it removes the terrifying unknown. Once you know you can handle the worst-case scenario, challenges stop feeling catastrophic and start feeling manageable.

- **Then, check in with future you:** When fear starts taking over, imagine yourself a year from now, looking back at this moment. What would that version of you want to tell you? It's usually something like "I'm so glad you didn't give up" or "that thing you were worried about didn't even matter."

Once you've tried this, other strategies may come into play, such as a favorite of Deb's to recommend to her coaching clients: Keep track of what's actually going *right*. Create a weekly evidence log documenting progress you've made, positive feedback you've received, problems you've solved, skills you've developed, and people who believe in your success. This isn't about false optimism but about balanced perspective. When you systematically collect evidence of your progress, it becomes much harder for anxiety to convince you that everything is falling apart.

> ### WHY WOMEN'S CAREERS LOOK DIFFERENT
>
> Women's career paths often don't look like men's because they can't. That's not a failure of women. The system creates different rewards and obstacles for us. Understanding that women's career paths often follow distinctive patterns can help you recognize you're not failing; you're navigating a system designed for different trajectories.
>
> Organizational psychologist Michelle P. King identifies three phases many women experience:[12]
>
> 1. **Idealistic Achievement (24–35):** Young women are achievement oriented and optimistic about their prospects. They can see the obstacles before them but are confident they can rise above them. Eventually young women come to realize that this meritocratic ideal isn't playing out in practice, chipping away at their self-belief.
> 2. **Pragmatic Endurance (36–45):** Women at this middle stage of their career are seeing their early expectations collide with reality. They may well find their rise up the corporate ladder to have stalled. Women start to feel dissatisfied and disenfranchised. During this phase, women endure inequality and impossible choices, with an emphasis on pragmatism. They perform a difficult juggling act, doing what they need to when they need to.
> 3. **Reinventive Contribution (46–60):** The good news is that the different shape a woman's career often takes comes with an upside. For women, this later stage can be one of new possibility, a time for reconceptualizing and reclaiming a woman's career. Earlier individualistic ambitions give way to a desire for respect and recognition, for the chance to live an integrated life, for opportunities to contribute to others and to society.

If you're in the pragmatic endurance phase and feeling stuck, what feels like failure might actually be the beginning of your most authentic chapter.

WHEN ORGANIZATIONS ACTUALLY HAVE YOUR BACK

Some organizations have figured out how to create psychological safety nets that help people navigate doubt instead of getting paralyzed by it. Dr. Amy Edmondson, a Harvard Business School professor, defines psychologically safe environments as those where people feel safe to take risks, make mistakes, ask questions, and admit when they don't know something. This isn't just a nice to have, Edmondson found; teams with psychological safety actually perform better because people aren't wasting energy covering up mistakes or avoiding challenges.[13]

Google discovered this with Project Aristotle, their study of what makes teams effective. They expected to find that the best teams had the smartest people. Instead, psychological safety was the single most important factor. The highest-performing teams were those on which people felt safe to fail, ask for help, and admit mistakes. When organizations create psychological safety, they also need to provide visibility of the recovery process.

As author Rachel Simmons points out, what women really need are "work-in-progress models" that go beyond achievements to show the struggle and bounce-back process. Seeing other women publicly succeed after setbacks helps normalize failure as part of the growth process.[14]

Dr. Joan C. Williams, distinguished professor of law at UC Law San Francisco and affiliated with Stanford's Women's Leadership Innovation Lab, suggests a way for women to be a safety net for each other when trying to self-promote without it backfiring on them: the posse solution.[15] Instead of self-promoting alone, women can strategically amplify each other's accomplishments in meetings and leadership discussions. This approach aligns with the Obama administration's amplification strategy, in which female staffers deliberately repeated and credited one another's ideas until they could no longer be ignored.[16]

Women can apply this in their workplaces via strategies like these:

- Publicly acknowledging each other's contributions in team settings
- Redirecting credit when it's misattributed or overlooked
- Advocating for colleagues' promotions and leadership roles

Even academic institutions are seeing the value in preparing women to fail—and to fail well. Rachel Simmons has what might be the best job title on any college campus: Smith College's failure czar. When she started the role, she discovered that these incredibly accomplished students had a problem: They'd been so successful getting into Smith that they had no idea how to handle even the smallest setbacks.

"We're not talking about flunking out of premed or getting kicked out of college," Rachel explained. "We're talking about students showing up in residential life offices distraught and inconsolable when they score less than an A– or ending up in the counseling center after being rejected from a club. Students who are unable to ask for help when they need it or are so fearful of failing that they will avoid taking risks at all."[17] Rachel understood because she'd been there. For years, she hid her own spectacular failure: dropping out of a prestigious scholarship program in her twenties after her college president told her she'd embarrassed the school. "For years, I thought it would ruin me," she admitted.

So she tried something different: Make failure impossible to ignore. Smith's Failing Well program puts students' and professors' worst moments up on big screens during orientation and finals weeks. Students share stories like "I failed my first college writing exam" and "I came out to my mom, and she asked, 'Is this until graduation?'" Faculty join in too: "I failed out of college. Sophomore year. Flat-out, whole semester of F's on the transcript."

Students were surprised by the honesty. "It was almost jarring," said student Carrie Lee Lancaster. "On our campus, everything can feel like such a competition. So to see these failures being talked about openly, for me I sort of felt like, 'O.K., this is O.K., everyone struggles.'"

Rachel also gives every student a certificate of failure that grants them permission to mess up. "What we're trying to teach is that failure is not a bug of learning; it's the feature," Rachel explained. "It's not something that should be locked out of the learning experience."

In our interview with Rachel, she told us she views the fear of failure that many young women struggle with as being rooted in a larger problem: the inability to tolerate discomfort. The real challenge, she says, is to reframe discomfort from something we need to fear or avoid to a signal we need to make a change.[18] It's exactly the mindset needed, whether in an organization or in ourselves, to help us all navigate our danger zone moments.

Key Takeaways

- **Navigate the danger zone with "not yet" thinking:** If you feel stuck, discouraged, or uncertain, that doesn't mean you're failing; it means you're in the process of figuring it out.
- **Create a failure plan:** Use the disaster scenario you're imagining to draft a concrete plan for what you'd do *if* the worst were to happen.
- **Use "so what?" thinking:** Check in with your future self to explore what about who you fundamentally are would change if you failed.

CHAPTER 8

Creating Your Failure-Safe Support System

When Reshma Saujani decided to run for Congress in 2010, she knew she was taking an enormous risk. As a first-generation American with no political experience challenging an entrenched incumbent, the odds were overwhelmingly against her. But Reshma understood something crucial about taking intelligent risks: Success isn't just about individual courage; it's about building the right support system to sustain that courage when things get difficult.

Before announcing her candidacy, Reshma spent months deliberately constructing what she calls a courage network.[1] She knew that running for office with no political background would inevitably lead to setbacks, criticism, and moments of self-doubt. Rather than face these challenges alone, she strategically assembled a diverse group of allies who could provide different types of support when her confidence wavered.

Her network included experienced political advisors who could provide strategic guidance, fellow risk-takers who understood the emotional challenges of ambitious goals, and trusted friends who believed in her vision even when polls showed her trailing significantly. Most importantly, she surrounded herself with people who viewed potential failure differently from how she had been conditioned to see it.

When Reshma lost the primary election, garnering only 19 percent of the vote, her carefully constructed support system proved invaluable. Instead of interpreting the loss as evidence she wasn't meant for public service, her network helped her extract crucial lessons from the experience. They reminded her that the skills she'd developed during the campaign (including public speaking, fundraising, and building coalitions) were transferable assets for future ventures.

This reframing proved prophetic. The relationships Reshma built during her congressional campaign became the foundation two years later for launching Girls Who Code, which has now reached over 450,000 women and girls globally. Many of the same people who had supported her political risk-taking became early investors, advisors, and advocates for her nonprofit venture.

"I've learned that bravery isn't a solo act. The women who take the biggest risks surround themselves with people who believe in their vision, especially when they don't believe in it themselves," Reshma wrote in her book *Brave, Not Perfect*.[2]

Reshma's experience illustrates a crucial principle: Building your failure-safe support system isn't just about having people to comfort you when things go wrong. It's about strategically assembling allies who will reframe setbacks as stepping stones, help you maintain perspective during challenging periods, and encourage you to take the next intelligent risk even when the previous one didn't work out as planned. The question isn't whether you need a support system; it's whether you're building one strategically or hoping it materializes when you need it.

WHY WOMEN NEED STRONG SUPPORT SYSTEMS

You don't have to take risks or face setbacks alone. In fact, you shouldn't. And for women navigating professional challenges, the right support system isn't just helpful; it's often the difference between bouncing back and staying stuck.

Women are less embedded in professional networks than men, which creates tangible disadvantages in negotiations, promotions, and career advancement.[3] Without access to key information and contacts, women often don't even know what opportunities exist. This network gap helps explain patterns we see in how women respond to setbacks.

Psychologist Froma Walsh describes relational resources as key to resilience: mentors and allies who provide guidance, peer support groups who normalize struggles, and family and friends who serve as emotional ballast during difficult transitions. Women with strong support systems don't just rely on personal grit. They systematically gather people around them who can offer different types of support. This isn't networking for networking's sake; it's strategic relationship-building that creates a safety net for taking risks and bouncing back from setbacks.

WHAT OUR SURVEY REVEALS ABOUT RESPONSE PATTERNS

But when setbacks actually happen, seeking support isn't always the first response. When we asked women how they typically react to workplace failure, we discovered five distinct response types. Some immediately blamed themselves and ruminated for days. Others withdrew completely. But some women took a different approach: They either sprang into problem-solving mode or actively sought support from mentors and peers. The difference wasn't in their circumstances; it was in their response strategy.

Of the people who shared their experiences, we found the following:

- 28 percent fell into self-blame and rumination, replaying events and losing sleep.

- 24 percent immediately shifted to problem-solving mode, regrouping and creating action plans.

- 19 percent actively sought support and perspective, reaching out to mentors and trusted advisors.

- 18 percent withdrew and shut down, retreating from opportunities and relationships.

- 11 percent immediately reframed failure as learning, the smallest but most resilient group.

The survey shows what women do when setbacks happen. But knowing what to do and actually doing it are different things. Here's what strategic support looks like in practice.

One executive in Fiona's Next Chapter Accelerator coaching practice was terminated unfairly, used as a scapegoat when the company needed someone to blame. Through their work together, Fiona helped her move from shock to strategy. "Fiona wouldn't let me stay stuck in the 'why me?' spiral," the executive recalls. "She had me map my entire network as different circles of support: close friends for emotional accountability, industry contacts for job leads, former colleagues who could vouch for my capabilities. She also coached me on how to tell my story without defensiveness—positioning myself as resilient, not damaged. And she made self-care nonnegotiable, not as a luxury but as fuel for clear thinking. That structure and reframing kept me from falling apart and helped me land a better role."

This story illustrates an important principle: Recovery requires more than resilience; it requires resources. So, what kind of resources? And how do you gather them, especially when you're in crisis mode?

SUPPORT IS A STRONG MOVE WHEN YOU'RE BOUNCING BACK

As Deb writes in her book *Go to Help*, when you try to handle everything yourself, you actually cut yourself off from people who want to help you. Plus, when you don't ask others for help, they may feel like they can't ask you for help either. You miss out on learning from others' expertise and experience.

Support shows up in different ways. Some women need mentors who've been through similar struggles. Others join groups in which people get what they're going through. Sometimes you need to change your environment entirely: leave a toxic workplace, redesign your role, build safeguards.

The bottom line: Building a strong support system isn't just nice to have. It's a strategic advantage that makes you more effective and more resilient.

BUILDING A PERSONAL BOARD OF DIRECTORS

Now that you understand the types of support that drive recovery, here's how to build your network.

Over the years, we've noticed something interesting: In our coaching work, we've noticed that those who navigate setbacks more successfully surround themselves with the right people. When you're facing a big career decision, who do you call? Sometimes we default to whoever's most available or closest to us rather than who's actually best equipped to help us think it through.

We've noticed three distinct roles that consistently show up in the support networks of women who push through challenges. Having a personal board of directors is different from simply having a network. This is a select group of people who actively help you make strategic career decisions. They can include the following:

- **Strategic Support:** This group includes thought partners who help you think through challenges, accountability buddies who keep you focused on your goals, and constructive critics who push you to improve.

- **Professional Advocates:** These supporters are sponsors who advocate for you when opportunities arise, defenders who stick up for you in your absence (or presence), and connectors who make introductions to people you should know.

- **Personal Champions:** These friends and colleagues are the empathizers who show care and compassion when you need them, cheerleaders who encourage you when things get hard, and caregivers who remind you to take care of your mental and physical well-being.

If you're navigating uncertainty or fear, curating a small trusted advisory group can make all the difference. You'll have a team invested in your success. Diversity matters here—you want varied perspectives, not an echo chamber.

DEB

Deb has a group of four friends (who all happen to be exceptional executive coaches) with whom she texts almost every day, gathers with via a group Zoom once a month, and sees in person twice a year. This is her core support team of strategic supporters, professional advocates, and personal champions. Deb never has to think, "Who can I go to for this?" because someone from this group will make themselves available on very short notice. She has turned to them for help with client challenges (strategic support), business development advice and introductions (professional advocates), and personal pep talks and guidance while writing this book (personal champions).

The women who successfully navigate career ups and downs have cracked the code on building a failure-safe support system. They've learned to be thoughtful about whom they invite into their inner circle when the stakes are high.

FROM CONTRIBUTOR STEPHANIE LEBLANC-GODFREY
40 ALLIES AND A STRETCH ASSIGNMENT

While building your personal board of directors is crucial individual work, organizations also have a responsibility to create structures that support women, especially women of color, in building these networks. One of the most comprehensive approaches we've seen is what Bonita Stewart calls 40 Allies and a Stretch Assignment.

In their book *A Blessing: Women of Color Teaming Up to Lead, Empower, and Thrive*, Bonita Stewart and Jacqueline Adams harken back to the largely broken promise made to freed slaves at the end of the Civil War: a chance to build new lives with the initial investment of forty acres and a mule. 40 Allies and a Stretch Assignment adapts this concept to surround a "rising star" employee of color with improved feedback, additional allies, and an opportunity to stretch and grow their capabilities.[4]

Forty allies may sound like a lot until you break it down:

- Ten people on your existing team at work
- Ten managers from other parts of the business
- Ten "sisters" or supportive women of color
- Ten members of your personal board of directors

This support may come from within your organization or outside of it, as we'll explore later. The power of this approach becomes clear when setbacks happen. With 40 allies already in place, a woman of color facing a career challenge has multiple people she can turn to for different types of support: teammates who understand the immediate context, managers who can advocate across the organization, peers who share similar experiences, and trusted advisors who provide strategic guidance. This isn't just about career advancement. It's about creating a safety net that makes it possible to take risks and bounce back when things don't go as planned.

BUILDING RELATIONSHIPS INTENTIONALLY

Most people wait until they're in crisis to build their support network. By then, it's too late to build the deep relationships that really matter.

The women who navigate setbacks most successfully don't wait until the breaking point to build support. They invest in relationships in advance—broad networks based on trust, connections with people who can provide visibility and opportunity.[5] When challenges come, they already have people to turn to.[6]

The most successful women we know think about relationship-building the way entrepreneurs think about product development: They're thoughtful and intentional. They identify what kind of support they need and then build those relationships over time. This doesn't mean being calculating or manipulative. It means being honest about what you need and generous about what you can offer in return.

Start by taking inventory of your current inner circle. Whom do you turn to when things get challenging? Which of these three roles are missing? Where are the gaps? Then think about where you might find people to fill those roles: professional associations, alumni networks, industry conferences, even your current workplace. The key is looking for people who have the characteristics you need and then finding ways to add value to their lives too.

Remember, the best support networks are built on mutual benefit, not one-way relationships. The goal is to create a group of people who all succeed together.

Key Takeaways

- **Ask for help:** Soliciting support doesn't make you look weak. It makes you look smart.
- **Build before you need it:** Build your support network before crisis hits, not during it.
- **Include three types of supporters:** Make sure you have strategic supporters (who help you think), professional advocates (who champion you), and personal champions (who sustain you emotionally).
- **Avoid the echo chamber:** Your board should include people with different perspectives, backgrounds, and experiences—not just people who think like you.
- **Be generous with your support for others:** If you've experienced failure (and we all have), you may be just the friend or colleague that someone else needs right now as they work on bouncing back.

PART 3

Bounce Back

Failure takes many forms and can come at us from many directions. Yet for all the variety of failure or setbacks—big or small, our doing or not—most of us experience similar emotions: shame, embarrassment, anger, anxiety, and sadness.[1]

That's not a bad thing. In fact, research shows that leaning into our feelings after failure is an important part of the coping process; it's how we learn and improve for the next time.[2] Therefore, it's critical to learn a set of tools that allow us to become emotionally intelligent about processing failure. By noticing our emotions and working through them in a deliberate and reflective way, we can move on from our default reaction and adopt a more proactive, adaptive response.

Through our combined years of professional experience, we learned what helps women recover from failure. Across cultures and industries, successful recovery followed a similar pattern: self-compassion, taking small actions, embracing new learning, and engaging peer support.

Based on our survey, interviews, research, and personal experiences with bouncing back from failure, the process we present in the following chapters is what we call The Three Gs: Ground, Gather, Go!: a three-phase framework for processing failure, gathering resources, and aiming high again.

CHAPTER 9

Ground

Author Elizabeth Gilbert was unable to write after her book *Eat, Pray, Love* became a global phenomenon. Despite having sold 12 million copies of her book—a book that launched a major motion picture—Elizabeth found herself emotionally and intellectually incapacitated. What if the next thing she wrote was a massive disappointment? In her TED Talk, "Your Elusive Creative Genius" (viewed over 17 million times), she described feeling like "a failure before I'd even begun."[1]

Her core identity as a writer felt vulnerable. Her livelihood felt threatened. She was stuck.

Here's what she didn't do: force herself to write. Here's what she did do: grounded herself in the present moment. She permitted herself to feel all her feelings, including grief and terror. She practiced "stubborn gladness," staying with her fear rather than trying to fix it or run away from it. In interviews with Oprah Winfrey and in her book *Big Magic*, Elizabeth describes her "conversation with creativity," in which she would literally speak aloud to her fear: "I see you, fear. I acknowledge you. But you don't get to drive."[2]

Elizabeth also decided that trying to write another *Eat, Pray, Love* was a recipe for frustration. Instead, she dedicated herself to writing what she was curious about rather than focusing on what would be a commercial success. The result? Her critically and commercially successful novel *The Signature of All Things*, written from a place of groundedness rather than fear.

GROUND YOURSELF IN THE MOMENT

Instinctively, we perceive failure as a threat. Our first impulse is to protect ourselves. But because the primitive part of our brain concerned with danger and threat bypasses our cognitive centers, those initial instincts might not be very productive. The majority of the women we surveyed experienced emotions like shock, shame, and anger after failure, followed by actions such as rumination, withdrawal, avoidance, and even fighting back.

Yes, we will likely feel defensive. We might feel the urge to blame ourselves or others. We might catastrophize and obsess about the consequences of our failure. We might shut down for fear of making matters worse. But left unaddressed, things can get worse. Our survey respondents shared that their failures led to insomnia, panic attacks, depression, illness, and even hospitalization.

All of these responses are rooted in regret about the past or fear of the future. The Ground phase of bouncing back is about now. It is, as cliché as it may sound, about being in the moment: standing on the ground of now, returning to yourself, to your body, to your emotions. It is about noticing—not judging, assessing, deciding, or taking action. That comes later.

If you want a simple rule to go by in this phase, it is this: no sudden movements. When in doubt, stop. Even if you're under pressure and need to act sooner than later, pause. Even if you're a problem-solver with a bias for action, pause. One of the things about failure is it can take a while for the full consequences to play out. When in doubt, take a wait-and-see approach. It may be helpful to visualize a speed bump, a yellow light, a yield sign, or a full stop sign.

MINDFULLY RETURN TO YOUR BODY

People often describe moments of distress or trauma almost as out-of-body experiences. You might feel as if you're observing yourself from a distance. In the case of failure, you might be wondering if this is really happening. Simply paying attention to the sensations of the in and out of our breath can do wonders.

Taking it a little further, Betty Erickson suggests what some call the 5-4-3-2-1 exercise:[3]

1. Name five things you see (the TV, a tree, a piece of paper, a dog, a pair of scissors).
2. Name four things you feel (the chair I am sitting in, the socks on my feet, the breeze from the fan, my feet on the ground).
3. Name three things you hear (a dog barking, the washing machine running, the fridge humming).
4. Name two things you smell (my dog's feet, cleaning spray).
5. Name one thing you taste (the gum I am chewing).

It may seem incredibly rudimentary. But simply taking the time to stop and tap into all of our five senses can ground us in the present and help us break out of the vicious cycle of anxiety. Taste and smell are especially powerful senses. Spend some time eating a bite of delicious food as slowly as you can, paying close attention to every aspect of the experience: the taste, the texture. Meditation leaders often guide students through a body scan, in which you start with your feet and move your way on up, noticing exactly what's going on from head to toe. Similarly, you can try to make small movements in every muscle of your body, one at a time. Or you can simply lie on your back on the floor, close your eyes, and listen to the beat of your own heart.

The goal of this simple practice is not just to return to the body and be in the moment but also to soothe and calm yourself.

PRACTICE SELF-COMPASSION

Self-compassion is a tricky concept. Any word starting with *self-* can seem . . . self-indulgent? Or at the very least, it might be tempting to see compassion for self and compassion for others as opposites. But as Kristin Neff, one of the foremost experts on the topic, points out, the two are actually flip sides of the same coin. Practicing self-compassion deepens our compassion for others. It gets us out of our self and our own head instead of trapped inside it.[4]

Kristin identifies three ways in which compassion for self and compassion for others share common ground:[5]

- **Kindness vs. Judgment:** When we allow our inner critic to take over, we are not being mindful of what we are feeling in the moment. And we can't practice self-compassion without first being acutely aware of the suffering we are experiencing. Moreover, judgment fast-forwards us into problem-solving mode, in which we want to fix things. You're not at that point in the process yet.

- **Common Humanity vs. Isolation:** Our initial fight-or-flight response to failure or any other threat is actually quite egocentric. We are very focused on *us*. It feels like something exceptional and abnormal is happening *to* us. Compassion for self and for others helps us see that mistakes and setbacks and suffering are not the exception but the norm.

- **Mindfulness vs. Overidentification:** Mindfulness is about getting close to the difficult feelings around failure rather than distancing ourselves through self-judgment, problem-solving, or numbing or distracting ourselves. But when we don't take the time to notice our feelings, we actually become more trapped in our heads and endlessly ruminate about the failure. We overidentify with it. Instead of saying, "I screwed up and it makes me feel like . . . ," we say, "I *am* a failure." That path leads nowhere but in circles.

A big part of all of the above is the simple practice of noticing and naming. Just as we notice the in and out of our breath during meditation or notice the sensations of our bodies during a body scan, the practice here is to simply notice (neutrally, without judgment, and with kindness if possible) what we are feeling—and then to put a name to it. The very act of naming feelings, research shows, reduces the raw hurt, settles us, and allows us to get out of our heads.[6] (This is why many refer to this method as "Name it to tame it.")

But self-compassion goes beyond naming and acknowledging the emotion. Treating ourselves with kindness allows us to create a different kind of conversation with ourselves that is more conducive to letting painful emotions dissipate.

GIVE YOURSELF PERMISSION TO GRIEVE

Grief can hit us at any point in the process. We might go straight to grieving our failure. Or it may take a while for us to fully come to terms with what has happened, with what we've lost, with what it's going to take to bounce back, with the difficult lessons we're going to have to learn.

If aiming high (and getting there) is the mountaintop, grieving is the descent into the valley, which makes it integral to the process of finding solid ground once again. It is when we deepen the work of noting and naming and sitting with our difficult emotions. It is also when we begin to lay the foundations for bouncing back.

Failing doesn't feel good, and neither does grieving the failure. It can be tempting to avoid or deflect those difficult experiences, especially if we define ourselves in terms of our drive and ambition.

Reviewing the five stages of grief that Elisabeth Kübler-Ross introduced is a helpful reminder that grieving is a process, and hardly a linear one. We may feel paralyzed by grief for a while and at times feel we're going backward rather than forward. That's okay. In the first shock of grief, we likely feel denial ("I can't believe this is happening") and then anger ("This is *not* happening to me!"). Bargaining ("What if I . . . ?") follows next, often accompanied by guilt. We bottom out with depression ("I am so, so sad"), a stage at which we may feel we're regressing, but these are important emotions to go through. Finally, we come to a full acceptance of our loss ("Here I am"), which comes with the ability to move on and to learn from the experience.

GRIEVING IS ALL ABOUT VALUES

Failure often threatens something deeper than a missed goal: our core values.

The facts of core values—what core values are and the role they play in our lives—may seem self-evident, but they're not. We tend to conflate values with virtue. But as historian Gertrude Himmelfarb writes, "Values, as we now understand the word, do not have to be virtues; they can be beliefs, opinions, attitudes, feelings, habits, conventions, preferences, prejudices, even idiosyncrasies."[8]

We may think that because our core values help define who we are, it should be obvious what they are. But that's not always the case. Some of our deepest core values might be unspoken, even unconsciously held. They can be an implicit rather than explicit presence in our lives. Then there are questions of alignment. Do we actually honor our values in word and in need? And do our stated goals mesh with our stated values? And how do our values get threatened when we've failed?

DEB

As an executive coach, I use values work to help my clients identify what's most important to them, what drives them, and what to do when values are in conflict.

I have found it useful to apply the lens of values work to my own life as well. When my coaching business was at risk of failing during the financial crisis of 2008, I wasn't worried about not being able to afford food or medical care for my family (although I realize that many others were). I was hurt because I valued seeing myself as an achiever and valued my role in supporting my family. Both were at risk.

Consider your last failure. Then take a look at the sampling of values below. Identify which of your values felt threatened because of your failure.

ACHIEVEMENT	IMPACT	RESPECT
BUILDING	INFLUENCE	SECURITY
COLLABORATION	INTEGRITY	SERVING
COMPASSION	LEADING	SHARING
COURTESY	LEARNING	SUPPORTING
CREATIVITY	MASTERY	TEAMWORK
EXCELLENCE	PROFESSIONALISM	TRADITION
EXPERIMENTATION	QUALITY	WINNING
FUN	RECOGNITION	

It's not just the failure itself that hurts; it's that a core value feels threatened, a core value that is integral to your identity. A part of who you are is under attack. As always, simply noting and naming the source of your pain are helpful. Which of these values was challenged, or questioned, or tested, or somehow undermined as part of the failure? Maybe you value teamwork, and a group collaboration fell flat. Or you value professionalism, and you were undermined by your boss in front of your whole team. Or you're a big fan of winning, and you just lost—big.

You can go further and turn the pain and loss into an affirmation. The fact that a failed collaborative effort hurts means you care deeply about teamwork. That's good! Furthermore, you can translate that sting into being resolved to pay even more attention to team dynamics the next time. You're still in the grieving stage—but you're already planting seeds for growing and bouncing back.

As much as it hurts—and in a sense, precisely *because* it hurts—moments of failure are a perfect time to do this kind of values work. Failure is almost by definition a goal that has, at least for the moment, gone south. And because grief so powerfully and painfully lets us know what matters to us, it can clarify whether our goals are aligned with our values.

WHAT ARE YOU GRIEVING?

The values work outlined above can help you clarify exactly what you are grieving: What has been lost? What is the cost or the harm? What are the (perceived) consequences?

With some failures, the feared loss might be reputational. When Deb was in elementary school, the greatest threat a teacher could lob at a student was "and this will go on your permanent record!" When we fail, we worry about that permanent stain. We worry about what colleagues and peers think. If the failure is public, we worry about our public reputation. We're also concerned about what people say about us on social media.

While having the veracity of our failure spread across Facebook or LinkedIn is one pain point, having it misrepresented cuts even deeper. If our failure elicits strong emotions in other people or infringes on their values, they're more likely to spread misinformation.[9] And, as research shows, any deviation from the true story is likely to spread "farther, faster, deeper, and more broadly" than the accurate version.[10]

Relatedly, we might be most concerned about having let others down. Especially when we feel our failure reflects on others who share our identity and, if we are a member of a marginalized community, that our failure may be seen as representative, we may grieve the perception that we played a role in stunting the progress of our community. Deb is quite used to hearing the question "but is it good for the Jews?" when news about other Jewish people's successes or failures hits the press. And when it's a failure of a Jewish person, it feels like the entire Jewish community has been let down.

Sometimes failure lands most pointedly as a disappointment in ourselves. We may not have performed as well under pressure as we would have liked. We might have to look ourselves in the mirror and admit, "I am not (yet!) the leader I would like to be."

This is also a good time to distinguish guilt from shame. Guilt is an emotion (a kissing cousin to regret) in which we recognize that something we did or didn't do was wrong or not aligned with our values or not up to our standards. The bad feelings (as long as we don't stew in them endlessly) are a reminder to do better and can be a healthy motivating force. By contrast, shame goes to our actual identity. We end up feeling bad not just for what we did but for who we are. We conflate (in an unhealthy way) the person and the problem. Guilt tells us that the action was wrong; shame tells us that *we* are wrong. And while guilt can hurt, shame can kill.

Practice self-compassion, and, with that critical adverb *yet*, give yourself the grace of being a work in progress. Separate your actions from your identity. Failing does not make you a failure.

MOURNING OUTCOME WHILE AFFIRMING PROCESS

In the immediate aftermath of a failure, everything about the experience feels bad. Parsing exactly what has (and what has not) been lost can lead to some important distinctions between outcome and process. When we are clearly responsible for the outcome, it might be appropriate to grieve both; a flawed process may have produced the poor outcome. But at other times, we might have done everything as well as we could, and the outcome was undermined by circumstances beyond our control or by a decision that wasn't ours to make. In those cases, we can find cause for hope in the process we followed, regardless of outcome.

YOU DON'T NEED TO GRIEVE ALONE

As Mary-Frances O'Connor points out in *The Grieving Brain*, grief is a feeling while grieving is a process whereby our relationship with that feeling changes over time.[11] You don't have to go through this process alone. Making a deliberate effort to communicate and connect with others can facilitate that evolving relationship with grief.

We get two things from seeking a shoulder to lean on. The first is simple commiseration: the act of someone sitting with us in the early stages of grief when we don't yet know how to respond or move forward. As the work of Bruce Perry (the psychologist perhaps best known for his collaboration with Oprah Winfrey, *What Happened to You? Conversations on Trauma, Resilience, and Healing*) has shown, when we are experiencing trauma of some sort, our rational and deliberate mind does in a sense go "offline."[12] So keep it simple. Practice self-soothing and self-compassion. Focus on activities with low cognitive demand. Just be present. You need the time and space to settle and ground and return to earth before you are ready to make key decisions.

Once we've processed the raw feelings of grief, it's time to make some sense out of the experience. Author David Kessler posits meaning as a sixth stage of grief.[13] This is the story we tell about our loss, what it means to us, how it has changed us, and how we envision our own life story going forward. Meaning-making and storytelling are inherently social activities. Engage others in this process. And remember that professional help is always an option.

PAIR GRIEVING WITH GRATITUDE

This may at first seem an odd pairing: Why should I be grateful for this failure that's making me so miserable? But remember: We only grieve over that which we care deeply about. Having work and ambitions that mean a lot to us is something to be grateful for in itself.

Using grief and gratitude in the same sentence makes more sense when we recall some of the funerals or memorial services we've attended. As difficult as they are, there is often a sense of celebration as well. There is a solid body of research supporting the idea that deliberately incorporating a gratitude practice into the grieving process contributes to our well-being, mediates the pain of loss, and increases our resilience.[14]

Deb shares this list of gratitude opportunities with her clients when they could use a reminder of the gifts they have, even in the face of grief:

I am grateful for . . .

- These friends
- These family members
- These colleagues
- These leaders
- These opportunities
- These challenges
- These people who make my life easier
- These privileges
- These simple pleasures

- These ways I am healthy
- These hopes
- These talents
- These life lessons
- These sources of laughter
- These values that I hold

Acknowledging what you have even when you feel like you're losing everything is a critical step in bouncing back from failure.

"Ground" Summary

Objective: Give yourself the time and space to process the emotional impact of the failure.

Action Steps:
- Practice no sudden movements.
- Practice self-soothing and self-compassion.
- Reflect on your core values.
- Keep perspective, and understand that setbacks are a part of life, not a reflection of your personal worth.
- Pair grief with gratitude.

CHAPTER 10

Gather

Sitting with the pain and disappointment of the cost of failure is an important step, but there's a thin line between giving grieving its due and dwelling on the past. If grief takes us to the lowest point in the valley, Gather is when we start summoning our resources and our inner strength for the climb up.

Patricia Obiero has always been a perfectionist. There was a positive side to that perfectionism: She had the strong will needed to fulfill the greatness she felt inside of her. On the other hand, her perfectionism masked fear. She knew, coming from Africa, and specifically from Kenya, she would face bias out in the world as she strove to compete on global platforms and establish herself as an expert. So at an early age, she said to herself, "Let me be perfect in everything I do."[1]

She looks back on the experience of growing up poor and realizes that she connected failure to poverty, as if poverty was a sign of failure. She felt she had to escape poverty and be at least comfortable in order to be listened to: "I was running away from poverty. And poverty was chasing me."

In her talk at the WILD Network Leadership FailLab, she spoke about how when you are running full speed ahead, driven by perfectionism, your vision is narrow. You aren't able to slow down and notice the people running alongside you. You can't pause to look sideways and see who might be able to help you.

She looks back and can now see clearly the stress and anxiety her perfectionism created for her. You can run toward perfection, but you will never get to it; it's always running away from you. Patricia had always been ambitious. But now she has found a boldness that allows her to move beyond fear.

PUT REGRET IN ITS PLACE

One of the first things we may need to gather to move forward from failure is a little perspective. Regret can make that a challenging task. Regret is about comparing that outcome with what might have happened had we acted differently or made a different choice. Yes, "could have, should have" negative thinking can be debilitating if we wallow in it. But as Daniel Pink points out in *The Power of Regret*, counterfactual thinking—the ability to imagine an alternative sequence of events—is uniquely human and a useful tool if deployed strategically. It can inspire us to improve, to course-correct, and to avoid repeating old mistakes.[2]

It can be helpful to reflect on your primary failure pattern(s) so that you start breaking your own cycle of regret and take back your sense of agency. Below are several strategies you can consider employing.

Concrete Regret (Missed Targets and Defeats)

Separate what is in your control from what isn't. While you have control over some inputs (your mindsets, your behaviors, your communication), you don't have control over all of the external variables (other people's behaviors, systemic challenges, moving targets) that impact your results.

Take time to acknowledge your efforts. Give yourself credit for the time, energy, effort, and bravery that you put into aiming high.

Showing up fully for opportunities—even opportunities that don't go your way—is worth celebrating.

And then, treat defeats as sources of data and mine the data for the next time. Ask yourself, "What can I learn from this?" and "What would I do differently next time?" rather than wallowing in the loss.

Circumstantial Regret (Trapped by Circumstances)

Use neutral language when labeling your circumstances. "Name it to tame it" is a simple but powerful practice to help you shift from regret to reality. Try saying something like "I was one of one hundred people who were part of the company's layoffs" (which is naming what happened without blaming or shaming yourself) rather than "I wasn't good enough to keep my job."

Remind yourself about past times you rose above circumstances. Remember how you shifted a painful pattern in your family? Remember when you recovered from a flood or other natural disaster? Remember how you kept your family financially afloat during a recession? You've done it before, and you can do it again.

Do a small thing. You might have circumstantial constraints, but that doesn't mean you're without agency or options. If you've lost your job, update your resume today. If you work with a toxic boss, take lunch away from your desk so you can have a mental break. If you're caring for an elderly parent, find someone who can help you with at least one task.

Perceived Regret (Worry About Others' Judgment)

Ask yourself who really matters in your life. Think about the people whose opinions truly make a difference to you. Chances are it's a small (but mighty) pool, and it doesn't include people who aren't committed to your success.

Define success for yourself. Get clear about what constitutes a win (or even satisfaction) for yourself. Consider this for your work, family, spirituality, finances, community, health, leisure, relationships, environment, etc. Write it down so that you can refer to it when someone else tries to define success for you.

Get vulnerable with people you trust. Share your fears, worries, concerns—and yes, failures—with people who have a stake in your well-being. You'll likely notice that the people you care about "judge" you with understanding, compassion, and care.

Identity Regret (Disconnection from Past Self)

Reflect on the consistency of your core values. Your circumstances may have changed. You may have changed. But chances are some of your core values have remained the same. Consider your through line of values that have withstood the test of time, like connection, learning, impact, family, integrity, justice, or service.

Celebrate change as a part of life. If you're no longer changing, then you're no longer growing. Acknowledge transitions as a natural, healthy, expected, and positive part of life. And then view your ability to navigate those transitions as a core strength.

Talk to your past self (really!). Have a conversation in your head, out loud, or in a journal with your past self. Ask her what she's afraid you'll forget about who she was and how she supported you. Ask her what she wants for your future that's even better than the past. Acknowledge how she helped you get from there to here, and thank her for the role she played.

Paralysis Regret (Avoiding Risk to Prevent Failure)

Rewrite your definition of failure. If you see failure as something terrifying to be avoided at all costs, you'll stay scared and stuck. Practice seeing failure as how you learn, grow, and improve. Chances are that most of the positive changes you've made in your life had an element of failure along the way.

Use your fear to find and fix weak spots. Let's say you've been asked to make a major presentation in front of a large, important audience. Ask yourself, "What's the weakest part of my presentation?" "What do I hope they don't ask me?" "What will I do if the technology fails?" And then, make a concrete plan to address these fears.

Treat risk-taking like a muscle. Your biceps aren't going to get any stronger if you don't exercise them, and neither will your risk tolerance. Each week, pick a small risk to take and just do it. Ask for a discount from your insurance company. Travel someplace solo. Try a new workout class. Send a cold email to someone you admire. Speak up in meetings where you usually stay quiet.

As Daniel puts it, "Regrets that hurt deeply but dissolve quickly lead to more effective problem solving and sturdier emotional health." The idea, he says, is to lean into regret and embrace it as a sharp stick rather than a leaden blanket. "When regret smothers, it can weigh us down. But when it pokes, it can lift us up."[3]

REFRAMING FAILURE AS GROWTH

To look at something difficult in a new light, it can help to gather a new vocabulary. If failure is inevitable, how do we make peace with it? The answer lies in reframing failure—not as an indictment of our abilities but as an opportunity to learn and grow.

For Tine Knott, the CEO of DAI International, a large global company that helps society and communities become more prosperous, success was "anything but linear."[4] She says she had long ago lost the "protective armor" many high-achieving women feel compelled to present.

Tine asserts a tough truth: "You can't always be the better version of yourself." She says that as a young woman, she learned lessons from the self-help books that were popular at the time that now feel wrong to her. These books emphasized a positive "girl boss" mindset—as if all you had to do was show up in the right frame of mind. Tine's contrarian take on that is, "Sometimes you are in a totally shitty frame of mind, but you still have to show up."

For leaders especially, Tine says, talking about failure is a delicate balancing act. On one hand, you want to be authentic and vulnerable. Tine is incredibly candid about the performative aspect of leadership, especially while coping with failure. The process has two sides: a private face and a public face. Failure hurts, so we all need a couple of trusted people in our lives we can go to and just "whine a little bit . . . It feels unfair and you've got to be able to get that out of your system with some people who really know you. Eventually you can say to yourself, 'Yeah, maybe you got screwed—but who cares?'"

This private coping with failure allows you to put a little more polish on your public coping. There is an art to packaging failure in a way that is useful and offers a way forward: a path for learning, a path toward being better.

The ability to effectively cope with failure doesn't come easy, and it doesn't come overnight, Tine says. You can't wait for the spectacular failures. You build resiliency by acknowledging and dealing with the small failures. Owning up to small failures requires letting go of false confidence and the need to prove yourself.

EMBRACE ACCOUNTABILITY

There are situations that require us to gather our courage and admit when we've made an error. Owning your mistakes is a critical part of turning failures into learning experiences. If blaming others and pointing fingers is a deflection of the tough truth of knowing that we screwed up, accountability is leaning into that tough truth. In a sense, it's externalizing the power of regret we just spoke of. It's saying, "I wish I had done better, but I didn't. Now, how do we fix this?"

Accountability thrives only when failure is framed as normal and human. When the possibility of failure is accepted as inevitable and as part of the process of taking chances and aiming high, people are more likely to step forward and own their mistakes. That not only clears the air and paves the way for moving forward and improving, but it also builds trust and is a way to model healthy vulnerability.

PAIR REFLECTION WITH APPRECIATIVE INQUIRY

In the face of failure, we may have to explicitly remind ourselves to gather the good that sits alongside the bad. Appreciative Inquiry is an approach to organizational change and leadership that focuses on identifying what is working and building on that, as opposed to fixing what's not working. *Appreciate* has a double meaning. It means to value; it also means to grow. *Inquiry* is about getting curious. In other words, Appreciative Inquiry is where we get curious about what we value in order to grow it.

The idea here is to broaden and build on what is already working for someone. Even in a failure, we can choose to acknowledge what we did well, what was working. A strength-based mindset can set the stage for a strategic pivot. Perhaps we failed because the venture or the position or our approach to it wasn't a good fit to our strengths. That could be a wake-up call that it's time to shift lanes. Acknowledging that we do some things better than others doesn't make us a failure. "Taking a strengths-based approach means we are bold enough to lean into discomfort in a search for better understanding," states a Gallup report. "It means even in the midst of defeat, we study pathways to victory. It allows us to stop trying to play every role and start investing more in our own personal bests."[5]

> **APPRECIATIVE INQUIRY EXERCISE**
>
> Here is an exercise to help you take an Appreciative Inquiry approach to failing:
>
> - Think about a time when you failed and grew or gained something from that failure.
> - What were the mindsets that helped you grow or gain something? (A mindset is a belief, thought, or perspective. It's invisible.)
> - What were the behaviors you engaged in that helped you grow or gain something? (A behavior is something you do that is observable and measurable. It's visible.)
> - Who were the allies who helped you?
> - What are you proudest of?
>
> Use this recollection of recovering from a past failure to remind you of helpful mindsets, behaviors, allies, and sources of pride that you can leverage this time.

KEEP PERSPECTIVE AND SEE THE BIGGER PICTURE

We can gather the various facets of ourselves to aid in grappling with failure. We are more than one thing. We can think of ourselves as having a portfolio of selves—an idea we first heard on Adam Grant's *WorkLife* podcast. As he puts it himself, "When people reject you, it helps to remember there's another you. Don't put all your eggs in one identity basket. Having a portfolio of selves is a source of resilience."[6] We would go further and say remember there are *multiple* other yous. The one of you who was rejected—or who failed—is only one of them.

On that same podcast (whose topic was "Bouncing Back from Rejection"), Adam talks about how we tend to get trapped in a blame binary: When a work or personal relationship fails and we are rejected or fired or broken up with, it's either "I was wrong and failed," or it was the other person's fault. But there's a third option: the dynamic of the relationship itself. Maybe neither party was to blame; maybe it was just a bad fit. He cites a study showing that attributing difficulty or lack of success to the relationship, as opposed to trying to pin it on one person or the other, mitigates negative emotions like self-pity and anger, and in fact helps motivate people to improve in the future.[7]

Sometimes the rejection really does have little to nothing to do with us. Sometimes it's completely out of our control. Someone made a decision that we might initially experience as a personal failure. But objectively, it doesn't necessarily reflect on us at all.

Finally, there's the perspective of time. Suzy Welch, an author, television commentator, and business advisor, has what she calls The Rule of 10-10-10 for approaching difficult problems for which it seems there is no easy solution that will please everyone. She asks herself, "What will be the consequences of this decision in 10 minutes? In 10 months? In 10 years?" Whether she's applying this lens to everyday decisions or to something more momentous like the impending failure of her own marriage, Suzy finds this brings much-needed perspective to matters that can seem overwhelming in the moment.[8]

GATHER YOURSELF, GATHER YOUR RESOURCES

When Deb was training to be a coach, one of the credos of coaching that really resonated with her was this: We see our clients as the experts of their lives—naturally creative, resourceful, and whole. And if they don't have a coach already, we advise them to be their own coaches. A great coach doesn't try to fix her clients' problems. Sometimes the biggest contribution a coach can make is simply to guide the client through a process of connecting to and leveraging the resources they already have. We believe that about our readers as well.

In the immediate wake of a failure, we will probably underestimate the extent of our resources and the depth of our own resourcefulness.

Take inventory of all of the things you have going for you as you prepare to rebound and move forward.

First, Gather Your People

Resist the urge to isolate yourself after a setback. While turning inward may well be the first stage of grieving, it has an expiration date; at a certain point, it turns into rumination.

The Gather stage of bouncing back from a failure is an ideal time to grow your relationships, your allies, your network, and your community. Women who may have been set up to fail, or who at the very least don't have support from the old guard in a company, often have to get creative in finding allies.

As you prepare to bounce back, it's time to get serious (and strategic) about building your network. Women need a dual approach to networking: maintaining a close (but not closed) inner circle while also building more eclectic and wide-ranging networks.[9]

The most successful women keep their networks fluid—refreshing them and at key inflection points emphasizing new strategic contacts over old ones.[10] Embrace randomness, and stretch boundaries and comfort zones.

In the Gather stage, it is time to look outward and assemble your support network:

- **Friends and Family:** These are people who can listen without judgment, who offer a safe space for you to express your emotions and your hopes (and fears) for the future, and who will honor your preferences for how much you wish to share.
- **A Counselor or Therapist:** A mental health professional can be helpful during the grieving stage but also later as you explore strategies for bouncing back.

- **A Coach:** A key pivot to make during the gathering stage is moving on from the reactive questions you will naturally ask at first ("What just happened?" "What does this failure say about me?") to more forward-looking and proactive ones ("What do I want moving forward?" "What is the narrative I am telling about myself?"). If you've had a career setback, consider hiring a career coach who assists with job search strategies, resume building, interview preparation—and rebuilding your confidence.
- **Support Groups:** Sharing experiences with others who understand your situation can provide a sense of community and reduce feelings of isolation. And if you don't find a group that meets your specific needs, consider starting one yourself. We promise that you're not the only one wrestling with your particular challenge.
- **Online Communities:** Deb belongs to social media groups in which she can both offer and receive support on a range of topics with which she has struggled, such as mental health and body image. These online forums can help you access a broader network of support and advice from people worldwide while also giving you the option to be anonymous if you choose.
- **Mentors:** If you already have a mentor, this is the time to reach out. Your mentor is there to offer you advice, feedback, and guidance, especially on career-related issues. They're here to provide you with valuable insights, help you navigate setbacks, and even open doors to new opportunities—when you're ready. Cultivate mentors and sponsors when times are good so you can turn to them in these moments.
- **Professional Networks:** As with social media, we'd much rather share good news and accomplishments with our peers. But don't hide from your networks after a failure. This is the time to lean in rather than opt out. These peers and industry leaders

have had their own failures, and these connections can help you normalize your experience—and even lead to new job opportunities and collaborations.

Then, Gather Your Practical Tools

As helpful and important as it is to surround yourself with the right kind (and right amount) of people, you may need to pull together additional resources to help you bounce back from a failure. And you might need more than you think.

In his book *The Premonition: A Pandemic Story*, author Michael Lewis highlights how Dr. Carter Mecher, the senior medical advisor for the Department of Veterans Affairs, Public Health, used a "Swiss cheese" approach to advocate for a multilayered mitigation strategy during the 2020 COVID pandemic. While social distancing, handwashing, and masking each had "holes" in their effectiveness, when stacked up, the holes covered each other to create more protective outcomes.[11]

When gathering your resources, you may notice that no single self-care strategy is enough. And that's okay. Try layering as many tactics as you need to reduce your anxiety, feel less overwhelmed, and alleviate your sadness.

- **Educational Resources:** Learning can spark a growth mindset more oriented to process than results. Look for courses, workshops, books, or webinars to build new skills, knowledge, and insights.

- **Financial Advisors:** You shouldn't catastrophize the financial impact of a failure, but neither should you ignore the financial implications. This may be the time to leverage the expertise of a financial advisor who helps you manage finances, create budgets, and plan for future financial stability. Their professional advice can reduce financial stress and help you make informed decisions for right now and for the future.

- **Spiritual Practices:** Whether something you do in community or on your own, spiritual practices can provide inner peace and a deeper sense of purpose during challenging times. Consider prayer, meditation, reading, or any other activity that gives you a helpful perspective, grounding, and connection. Being in touch with your values and beliefs can provide strength and direction.

- **Movement:** Regular physical activity can improve mood, reduce stress, and enhance overall well-being. Consider joining a gym, fitness class, or sports team to stay physically active. Or if you're like Deb, you can count walking your dog, dancing to '80s hits in the privacy of your home, and active gardening as your fitness routine.

- **Creative Outlets:** Creative expression can be therapeutic and help process emotions related to failure. If you're thinking to yourself, "I'm not creative . . . ," tell your inner critic to pipe down. (Deb worked with a therapist who had a painting in her office that read, "Your inner critic is a fucking liar," which was a great reminder.) Engage in activities such as writing, painting, drawing, dancing, cooking, playing a musical instrument, rearranging your furniture, or even buying a new bold lipstick to express yourself and find relief from stress.

- **Visible Wisdom:** Perhaps you have a favorite quotation that you keep coming back to. Or you once got a piece of advice that has withstood the test of time. Or you have a mantra that has meaning or an object or artifact that gives you strength. Whatever it is that imparts wisdom, inspiration, or strength, now is the time to remember it and make it visible. Put your favorite quotations on Post-it notes, and stick them on your bathroom mirror. Make your mantra your new password. Make a playlist of songs that remind you of your healthy perspective (don't forget to include Gloria Gaynor's "I Will Survive"). Deb's friend Marc gave her a small stuffed "vulnerability turtle" that she keeps on a shelf in her office and can easily grab and squeeze whenever she needs it. (And she needs it.)

By gathering, layering, and leveraging these resources, you can build a comprehensive plan that addresses emotional, social, practical, intellectual, financial, spiritual, physical, and creative needs. This holistic approach can significantly enhance your ability to recover from setbacks and thrive in the face of challenges.

WHAT'S STOPPING YOU FROM CHANGING?

Gathering our resources is important. But if we try jumping back in the game again without first looking deep within and confronting some of the mindsets and behaviors that might have contributed to failure, we could be setting ourselves up to repeat the same old mistakes again. Looking at ourselves in the mirror and summoning the courage to change is hard work.

Robert Kegan and Lisa Lahey's Immunity to Change model can help us break through hidden barriers that prevent us from aiming high in the first place. *After* a failure, the need to confront difficult but necessary changes comes into even sharper focus. We've fallen short, and we don't want to repeat the same mistakes. But we also know that the human brain gets stuck in old habits. Walking ourselves through the four-step process can be a useful exercise at this point:[12]

1. What is your stated commitment, the thing you would like to change?

2. What are you doing (or not doing) that keeps this stated commitment from being realized?

3. What is the competing commitment—in other words, what about the status quo works for you, or works well enough that you are reluctant to let it go or mess with it?

4. What is the big assumption—the hidden motivation, the hidden belief—behind this competing commitment?

Understanding *why* we're stuck is a critical first step. Getting to the core of *what* is contributing to our being stuck is an insightful second step. Organizational psychologist Tasha Eurich has identified another root cause of why it can be so hard for us to change—specifically, why it's so hard for us to learn from the past. Her focus is on the art of self-awareness, which she defines as our ability to know who we are, how others see us, and how we fit in the world. She and her research team have found that while 95 percent of people rate themselves as self-aware, in fact only 10 percent to 15 percent are. (She calls them self-awareness unicorns.) The problem, she says, is that most people go about introspection the wrong way. We ask *why?* questions—which, because of their open-ended nature, essentially lead us to make stuff up.[13] Motivation is tricky, elusive, and largely subconscious. It's unknowable. *Why* questions also invite us to look in the rearview mirror, which can encourage rumination.

Tasha found that her self-awareness unicorns didn't ask, "Why?" They asked, "What?" Their introspection was about probing things that were specific, knowable, and actionable. *What* questions can point us toward skills or learning gaps that will equip us to succeed the next time around. For example, she talked to a man who was unhappy in his current career. He didn't ask, "*Why* do I feel so terrible most of the time?" Instead, he asked, "*What* are the situations that make me feel terrible? And *what* do they have in common?" One small word change. A world of difference.[14]

Even after we've identified the what that needs to change, how we frame the what can make a world of difference.

DEB

For years, I struggled to come up with an exercise routine that would help me lose weight. Then I shifted the goal to the side: The objective wasn't to exercise in pursuit of a different body; the objective was simply to move in pursuit of better mental and physical health. Moving was a more forgiving and malleable goal. It included walking with my dog Nash. It included taking small local hikes with friends. It included dancing to '80s music in the privacy of my office. Framing the hoped-for change differently was a small but effective shift.

BLIND SPOTS, HARD SPOTS, AND SOFT SPOTS

We know firsthand that it can be challenging to look at ourselves and see how we're getting in our own way. And this process can take months, years, and even decades! But for those of us who are short on time—and ready to make changes now—here's a quick model to help reflect on what's stopping us and start leaping forward:

- **What are your blind spots?** The writer Junot Díaz says, "We all have a blind spot, and it's shaped exactly like us."[15] And because we are the ones who get in the way of our ability to see the world (and ourselves) clearly, we need to turn to others. But who we ask for feedback and how we ask for that feedback are critical. It is all too easy to seek out the kind of answers we want to hear. What we really need are what Tasha calls loving critics—people who root for us and want the best for us but are also willing to give it to us straight.[16] Here's a great technique for leaders who want the unvarnished truth from their team: Walk into a meeting and ask, "Tell me something I don't want to hear."

- **What are your hard spots?** These are the areas in which we are stubbornly resistant to change; ingrained habits and patterns that we've accepted are simply hardwired in us. It's just who we are—except that each of us is actually more changeable and evolvable than we assume. An especially tricky part of hard spots is that they are often an outgrowth of our strengths. They are an overused strength that we lean on and default to uncritically, calling on them even when it's not appropriate. A pair of great questions to ask that might reveal your hard spots is, "In critical situations, what do I always do? What do I never do?" Such questions can be the start of identifying and breaking out of stale patterns.

- **What are your soft spots?** These are tender spots, like a bruise, that get activated when pressed. When someone tells you (or you tell yourself) that you need to be different in this area, it hurts. But, also like a bruise, soft spots can be sites of change and healing—particularly if we can find a new way of looking at the core issue. For example, Deb had always been told she was an attention seeker. It rang true, but it also stung. It sounded selfish. And as she became more well-known in her field, she wrestled with actually having so much attention. So she decided to redefine this core attribute. She wasn't seeking attention as much as she was seeking connection. That reframing helped her turn an enduring emotional wound into less of a pain point and more of a positive attribute.

- Sometimes an examination of our limitations brings us straight back to the question of values. Deb assumed that in order to build a successful business, she had to scale. And she loves collaborating with others, so she took on a team. Then she discovered she didn't like having a team she had to manage and oversee on a daily basis. She realized she valued her autonomy more than teamwork. She loves the collaboration of partnering with others on a specific project—but that's different from building and sustaining a team. A strategy that didn't work helped her clarify her values, her limitations, and her strengths.

AMENDS, REPAIRS, AND BRIDGES

If your failure has brought about some harm or discord or fractured a relationship, then it's important to try to make amends, repair relationships, improve trust, and build or rebuild bridges. You begin with embracing accountability and with an apology if needed. But it doesn't stop there—you can't just fast-forward from apology to redemption!

The hard work in the middle comes with the effort to see exactly what harm has been done, to understand more fully what mistakes or oversights or blind spots got you there, and then to try to rectify the situation by making the necessary repairs and putting in place practices that prevent a repeat.

Let's be clear: This is really, really hard. It carries an additional risk of failure if you aren't able to mend relationships and restore trust. You are making yourself vulnerable, which is a risk in and of itself. You are committing yourself to change. You are going to learn a lot about yourself and about the people around you.

There's a great line in the movie *Black Panther*: "In times of crisis, the wise build bridges while the foolish build barriers."[17] During a crisis, especially one of our own making, the impulse to retreat and adopt a bunker mentality is understandable. You may think to yourself "I've already screwed up once—why compound the situation by risking further mistakes?" And yet paradoxically, crisis and failure are perfect times to build relationships, bridges, and community. Like any disruption, they are times of fluidity, uncertainty, and discovery.

"Gather" Summary:

Objective: Lay the foundation for climbing out of the valley and bouncing back. Summon the resources, inner and outer, that you'll need to aim high again.

Action Steps:

- Engage in reflection and appreciative inquiry.
- Embrace accountability.
- Maintain perspective, and see the big picture.
- Gather yourself; gather your resources.
- Assess what's stopping you from changing.
- Make amends, and build bridges.

CHAPTER 11

Go!

French figure skater Surya Bonaly struggled to be judged fairly as a Black woman in a mostly white sport and as someone with a distinctive athletic style that featured ambitious and powerful jumps in contrast to the more restrained "artistic" style favored by traditionalists and many judges. For three consecutive years, she narrowly missed a gold medal in the World Championships. In the second of those years, in 1994 in Japan, she felt she had made concessions to the judges: no longer trying to land quadruple jumps, improving her gracefulness, and cutting the thickly braided ponytail she felt the judges didn't like. She finished in a tie with home country favorite Yuka Sato, losing in a tiebreaker. Feeling that even her best would never be enough, Surya stood beside the platform at the awards ceremony, later removing her silver medal. She was judged to be a sore loser.[1]

After losing the World Championships again in 1995 (by a mere tenth of a point), Surya had one last chance at an Olympic medal in 1998. Still recovering from a ruptured Achilles tendon, she had to depart from her planned routine. And when she failed a landing midway through and realized her chances of medaling were gone, she threw caution to the wind. She performed a backflip—technically banned in competition because it was deemed unsafe, and because it was supposedly impossible to land on one foot in the graceful manner in which all other figure skating jumps are traditionally performed. Surya landed it—to the dismay of the judges and the delight of the crowd. And she did so gracefully on one foot, the first and only Olympic skater to land a backflip on one blade.[2] After she completed the program, she turned her back on the judges and faced the crowd. She was competing for herself, for her fans, and by her own rules.

Surya continues to lead and inspire others as a full-time skating coach at the Shattuck-St. Mary's Figure Skating Center of Excellence (COE) in Faribault, Minnesota.[3] And like Surya, you have a comeback story in the making.

Now it's finally time to aim high again. But that doesn't necessarily mean reloading and taking another shot at what didn't work before. Aiming high again can be a lot of things. It might be soldiering through and turning what could have been a failure into a success. It could mean pivoting into something new and unfamiliar. Or it could be finding the opportunity in rejection or failure.

Failure is an investment, says Amy Edmondson: "You've paid for it, so you might as well reap the rewards."[4] This phase is when the returns from that investment start trickling in. Bouncing back and aiming high (again!) are one reward. So is the personal and professional growth you experience as you process, recover from, and learn from failure and find new inner strength, become more resilient, and build and deepen relationships.

None of that happens without a lot of work. If failure is a kind of wake-up call, a signal of things we need to change or correct, here is where we start to heed that call and put in practice a strategy for being better.

YOUR MILEAGE MAY VARY—A WORD ON TIMING

As we hope we've made abundantly clear, The Three Gs don't represent a formula or a template. There is no magic sequence. And there is no set timeline. Your time to Go! may come sooner than later, or later than sooner. We've spoken to women who took years to bounce back from failure. We hope that normalizing failure and giving you some tools to create a healthier relationship with failure will shorten that turnaround time. But if not, so be it.

Sometimes our moment to Go! again arrives sooner than we think and from an unexpected direction. One of WILD Network's Leadership FailLab participants, Carla Chamoun, felt she had flunked at handling the stress of being an ambitious professional who was also now a new mother, and she walked away from a job in banking. Her plan was to commit wholeheartedly to becoming the perfect mother, the perfect wife.[5]

From the start, the plan didn't work. Carla didn't like to cook; the kitchen was not a place where she thrived. She didn't know how to spend her days. But a few months into this failed experiment, she saw a job notice about a development nonprofit looking for someone with a background in finances. She'd come from the for-profit banking world, and this didn't exactly seem like a good fit. But she felt she probably had the right skill set. On impulse, she sent in her CV.

Carla was shocked to get a call back. She went in for an interview, during which she was asked whether she could do the job. She pointed to her CV: You can see my skill set, my track record. You'll have to decide if I can do the job.

She got the job and never looked back. She figured out a way to stop trying to be the perfect mother, only the best mother she could be while still pursuing her professional ambitions and doing what she loved to do. And she figured out a way to get her family to accept that. She hadn't made a plan. She hadn't gone through a deliberate process of slowly getting ready to bounce back. A voice inside her had said, "Go!" and she had listened.

FIDDLE WITH THE VARIABLES

After a failed experiment or an early iteration of a product that gets mixed reviews, scientists and innovators don't throw up their hands in despair. They isolate the multiple variables involved and start fiddling with them: Adjust here, tweak there, try again. Maybe your basic plan was solid, but you need to fiddle with who you partner with. So go again, but go with someone else. Maybe you need to extend the timeline or compress it. So go again, but at a different pace.

Each variable is a lever, a potential experiment, a chance to learn and discover. By shifting into the mode of the scientist and the experimenter, you also adopt a more process-oriented mindset. You define success in terms of process, effort, learning, and growth—not outcome.

LESSONS FROM *LOSERS*: PREPARE FOR YOUR COMEBACK STORY

The Netflix show *Losers* is a docuseries profiling athletes who have turned crushing defeats into positive experiences. Producer Mickey Duzyj felt that the sports and entertainment world focused disproportionately on winners: "It always struck me that everybody says that we learn more from our failures than we do from our victories, but that doesn't always manifest in popular culture."[6] The show is distinctive for its willingness to address issues of mental health, for framing spectacular defeat as an opportunity for self-reinvention, and for its acknowledgment of the power of community.

Mickey brings a unique lens to failing—and to bouncing back. For all of the apparent embrace of failure as opportunity in recent years, he points out that it is almost always "within the context of it being a temporary setback toward ultimate success."⁷ This was not the case for the subjects of *Losers*. They never bounced back in the sense of ultimately triumphing in the endeavor at which they had first failed. Rather, their bouncing back came in the form of a second act in which they found the freedom of playing by their own rules.

SET SMARTER GOALS

As award-winning writer, actor, and comedian Tina Fey puts it, "You can't be that kid standing at the top of the waterslide, overthinking it. You have to go down the chute."⁸ But going down that chute should be about velocity rather than speed. While speed is about the distance you travel over time, velocity adds direction into the equation; it moves you toward a goal.

If you're going to put the time, energy, and effort into setting a new goal or revisiting your previous goal, then go for an upgrade from the standard SMART goals model.

Quick recap: SMART stands for Specific, Measurable, Attainable, Realistic, and Time-bound. And there's nothing wrong with following that model. It works. But it's not inherently exciting, or compelling, or activating.

SMARTER stands for Systemic, Motivating, Aspirational, Resonant, Timely, Energizing, and Right. Let's look at each one:

- **Systemic:** Your goal should fit into the overall system—the big picture—of your life. Questions to ask yourself include, "What do I want? What other parts of my life will this impact? How does this fit into my vision for my life?"
- **Motivating:** Your goal should bring you closer to something you want. Ask yourself, "What do I want? What about this goal feels motivating? What part(s) am I looking forward to most?"

- **Aspirational:** Your goal should raise the bar: "How does what I want differ from what I have now? Who will I be when I accomplish this? What makes this a leap forward?"

- **Resonant:** Your goal should align with who you are and what you care about. Think about the following: "How does this goal align with my values? What speaks to me about this goal? What about this goal feels *so* me?"

- **Timely:** Your goal should be coming at a good time for you. Ask yourself, "Why now? What makes this a great time to tackle this? What makes it urgent or important?"

- **Energizing:** Your goal should fuel you. Consider: "Where's my energy for working on this coming from? How will I keep my energy for this goal alive? Who else has energy for this goal who I can partner with?"

- **Right:** The goal should come from a place of integrity. Reflect on these questions: "What about this goal feels right for me? How can I make this goal the right size for myself? How is this the right thing for now or the future?"

When you're ready to Go! ahead with your goal, make sure it's a goal that doesn't just whisper to you. It should be shouting your name!

ASK FOR THE KIND OF HELP YOU NEED

One of Deb's first jobs after graduate school was teaching fundraisers how to ask for money for the philanthropic causes they cared about. A key point of this training was letting these solicitors know that not everyone would want to or be able to give money—and that was okay. Making a donation was one way to help but not the only way. If someone wasn't prepared to be a donor, they could also help by being a door opener (make introductions to other people who might be able to support the cause) or a doer (roll their sleeves up and do some hands-on work for the mission). This meant that just about anyone who wanted to help could help—as long as they were being asked for the kind of support they could give.

When you're getting ready to Go!, you don't need to go it alone. You shouldn't go it alone. This is the time to reach out to your personal and professional networks to request the kind of support that will help you take your next small steps—or giant leap.

But before you do that, think about what kind of help would serve you so that you can make specific requests. In their book *Go to Help*, Deb and her coauthor (and daughter), Sophie Riegel, share that a broad, general request like "I could use some help!" decreases the likelihood that someone will help you. It leaves too much up to the other person's interpretation of what you actually need.[9]

Here are some starter ideas on specific things you might ask someone to do:

- Listen without judgment
- Empathize
- Problem-solve
- Brainstorm
- Share their experience
- Show you how to do it
- Push you beyond your comfort zone
- Remind you how awesome you are
- Help you stay focused
- Give you timely feedback
- Set some deadlines
- Celebrate your wins

And remember that a successful request for help includes knowing what kind of help someone is able to give. Don't ask your least compassionate friend for a shoulder to cry on or your most optimistic friend to play devil's advocate. Make it easy for your helpers to help you.

CELEBRATE WINS OF EVERY SIZE

Whether you notice a small glimmer of hope after a seemingly hopeless setback, get your first win on the path to a bigger victory, or have silenced your judgy inner critic for a few hours (or minutes), it's time to celebrate.

And that means . . . cocktails! When we celebrate, our brains release a "cocktail" of dopamine, oxytocin, and endorphins that help us feel happy, content, appreciative, fulfilled, resilient, purposeful, and connected to others.[10] We experience less stress and pain—even during periods of high pressure.[11]

And when we celebrate with others, those benefits are multiplied and magnified.[12]

Nevertheless, we often find celebrating our wins of any size challenging. According to research by psychologist BJ Fogg, founder and director of the Behavior Design Lab at Stanford University, "adults have many ways to tell themselves 'I did a bad job' and very few ways of saying 'I did a good job.'"[13] Our negativity bias wires us to look for bad, dangerous, and negative threats (as an evolutionary means of survival),[14] so we must be intentional about uncovering what's worth celebrating.

If you're a classic overachiever or a recovering perfectionist, you might be waiting to celebrate until you believe you deserve an A+. Should a "not there yet" or "still working on it" be considered a win? Yes, it should, especially if you want to motivate yourself to keep going.

Lowering the bar for a victory doesn't mean lowering your standards for yourself. It can mean raising your awareness of what's working well and increasing the chance you'll do more of that.

Here's how to celebrate your wins along the way:

1. **Celebrate the practice, not just the performance**: Think about a toddler learning how to walk. They typically do more stumbling than actual walking, and yet we clap and cheer for them with each attempt. Rather than waiting until you reach your destination, give yourself credit for the fact that you're putting one foot in front of another and getting better, stronger, and closer along the way.

2. **Celebrate in a way that feels meaningful to you**: You might be a "brunch with friends" kind of celebrator or a "quiet walk in the woods" celebrator. This is your win. Do what makes you happy. (Deb's family tradition is to have a Carvel ice cream cake for every win, large or small.)

3. **Thank anyone who supported you**: Your victory isn't diminished by having help along the way. Multiply the positive impact of your win by sharing it with others who have been on your team through the ups and downs. Let them know specifically how they contributed to what you're celebrating. A little positive reinforcement can go a long way.

4. **Deconstruct what you did well**: While you might have had some luck along the way, you also contributed helpful attitudes, beliefs, behaviors, allies, habits, and skills to this. Take time to reverse engineer your success. And yes, you can also reflect on what you could have done more of, less of, or differently—but don't let that dim the shine of what you've accomplished.

5. **Decide what you'll need to do to maintain your goal achievement or take it to the next level**: You've made it this far, and you're not done. Turn your successful approaches into habits, and apply those habits to the next phase of your goal.

"Go!" Summary:

Objective: Aim high again.

Action Steps:
- Embrace unexpected timing.
- Fiddle with the variables.
- Prepare for your comeback story.
- Set SMARTER goals.
- Ask for the kind of help you need.
- Celebrate wins of every size.

CONCLUSION

From Fearing Failure to Failing Forward

Our journey began with an acknowledgment of a fundamental truth: Failure hurts. And failure tends to strike women at our core, contributing to feelings of inadequacy, worries about belonging, and concerns about our future potential. As a result, we withhold our ideas and avoid taking essential risks in pursuit of our goals.

And the good news is this relationship with failure is neither inevitable nor permanent. When we acknowledge our missteps and create psychological safety for others, we build stronger, more innovative leaders and teams around us. And for us personally, our neuroplasticity allows us to rewire and rewrite our responses to failure, moving from threat to learning opportunity.

Chances are you've heard the age-old question, "What would you do if you knew you would not fail?" We invite you to consider this instead: "What would you do if you knew that failure was a healthy, productive, and necessary part of success?"

The world needs women like you who are willing to take risks, set bold goals, and use failure as a growth opportunity—not just for themselves but for the women (and allies) around them. Remember that your past failures aren't predictive of future failures; they are sources of wisdom, insights, and resilience.

So aim high, bounce back, and keep going.

You've got this. And we've got you.

Acknowledgments

Writing a book is never easy, and we are grateful to everyone who helped lighten the load for us. Thank you to Lee Reed Zarnikau for championing this project and for your exceptional edits and guidance. We are also grateful to the entire production team at Greenleaf Book Group for shepherding our book from birth to finish. We want to share a special thank-you to Scott Doyle, who helped us find our voice and shape our message at the very beginning. To the colleagues, mentors, and experts (too many to name—but they're named in this book) who shared their knowledge, stories, and experiences with us, we are deeply grateful. For everyone who contributed to the research in our survey, we want to thank you and let you know that we see you. We are lucky to have so many wonderful friends who supported us along the way. And finally, to our families, who always knew we could do this, your patience, encouragement, pep talks, and snacks helped us more than we can say.

Notes

INTRODUCTION

1. Fiona Macaulay and Deborah Riegel, "Fear of Failure in Professional & Personal Life Research Insights," survey conducted April 2024.
2. Elizabeth Day, *How to Fail* (Fourth Estate, 2020), 2–3.

CHAPTER 1

1. Fiona Macaulay and Deborah Riegel, "Fear of Failure in Professional & Personal Life Research Insights," survey conducted April 2024.
2. Fiona Macaulay interview of Stephanie Cohen, May 9, 2025.
3. Naomi I. Eisenberger and Matthew D. Lieberman, "Why Rejection Hurts: A Common Neural Alarm System for Physical and Social Pain," *Trends in Cognitive Science* 8, no. 7 (2004): 294–300, https://doi.org/10.1016/j.tics.2004.05.010.
4. Katty Kay and Claire Shipman, *The Confidence Code: The Science and Art of Self-Assurance—What Women Should Know* (Harper Business, 2014), 45–49.
5. Carol S. Dweck, *Mindset: The New Psychology of Success* (Random House, 2006), 205.
6. Alice H. Eagly and Steven J. Karau, "Role Congruity Theory of Prejudice Toward Female Leaders," *Psychological Review* 109, no. 3 (2002): 573–598, https://doi.org/10.1037/0033-295X.109.3.573.
7. Bonita C. Stewart and Jacqueline Adams, *2021 US Women of Color in Business: Cross-Generational Survey*, accessed June 5, 2025, https://leadempowerthrive.com/research2021.
8. Stewart and Adams, *2021 US Women of Color in Business: Cross-Generational Survey*, New York.

9. Bonita C. Stewart and Jacqueline Adams, *2020 Women of Color in Business: Cross-Generational Survey*, accessed June 5, 2025, https://leadempowerthrive.com/research2020.
10. Leon Festinger, *A Theory of Cognitive Dissonance* (Stanford University Press, 1957), 1–24.
11. Brené Brown, "Shame vs. Guilt," From Brené, Brené Brown, January 15, 2013, https://brenebrown.com/articles/2013/01/15/shame-v-guilt/.

CHAPTER 2

1. Diane Tsai et al., "Christine Lagarde Calls Out People Who Use Double Standards," *Time*, April 21, 2016, https://time.com/4300107/christine-lagarde-time-100-video/.
2. Katty Kay and Claire Shipman, *The Confidence Code: The Science and Art of Self-Assurance—What Women Should Know* (Harper Business, 2014), 8, Kindle.
3. Emily O'Donnell, "The Confidence Gap in Work Performance Reviews Between Women and Men," Wharton Stories, The Wharton School, January 3, 2020, https://www.wharton.upenn.edu/story/the-confidence-gap-in-work-performance-reviews-between-women-and-men/.
4. "Why Are There More Male Entrepreneurs Than Female Ones?" *Knowledge at Wharton* podcast, December 14, 2015, https://knowledge.wharton.upenn.edu/podcast/knowledge-at-wharton-podcast/why-are-there-more-male-entrepreneurs-than-female-ones/.
5. Lin Bian et al., "Gender Stereotypes About Intellectual Ability Emerge Early and Influence Children's Interests," *Science* 355, no. 6323 (2017): 389–391, https://doi.org/10.1126/science.aah6524.
6. Lisa Damour, "Why Girls Beat Boys at School and Lose to Them at the Office," *New York Times*, February 7, 2019, https://www.nytimes.com/2019/02/07/opinion/sunday/girls-school-confidence.html.
7. Women in Sport, "More Than 1 Million Teenage Girls Fall 'Out of Love' with Sport," news release, March 7, 2022, https://womeninsport.org/news/more-than-1-million-teenage-girls-fall-out-of-love-with-sport/.
8. Thekla Morgenroth et al., "The Gendered Consequences of Risk-Taking at Work: Are Women Averse to Risk or to Poor Consequences?" *Psychology of Women Quarterly* 46, no. 3 (2022): 257–277, https://doi.org/10.1177/03616843221084048.
9. Luisa Alemany et al., "How the Gender Balance of Investment Teams Shapes the Risks They Take," *Harvard Business Review*, December 24, 2020, https://hbr.org/2020/12/how-the-gender-balance-of-investment-teams-shapes-the-risks-they-take.
10. Paola Cecchi-Dimeglio, "How Gender Bias Corrupts Performance Reviews, and What to Do About It," *Harvard Business Review*, April 12, 2017, https://hbr.org/2017/04/how-gender-bias-corrupts-performance-reviews-and-what-to-do-about-it.
11. Julia Belluz, "Women Surgeons Are Punished More Than Men for the Exact Same Mistakes, Study Finds," *Vox*, November 23, 2017, https://www.vox.com/science-and-health/2017/11/23/16686532/surgeon-mistakes-gender-wage-gap.

12. Dayna Evans, "The Media Disproportionately Blames Women CEOs for Company Problems," *The Cut*, November 16, 2016, https://www.thecut.com/2016/11/the-media-blames-women-ceos-for-company-problems.html.
13. Michael Blanding, featuring Mark L. Egan, "Women Receive Harsher Punishment at Work than Men," Harvard Business School, Working Knowledge, Diversity and Inclusion, December 17, 2018, https://www.library.hbs.edu/working-knowledge/women-receive-harsher-punishment-at-work-than-men.
14. Julia Belluz, "Women Surgeons Are Punished More than Men for the Exact Same Mistakes, Study Finds," *Vox*, November 23, 2017, https://www.vox.com/science-and-health/2017/11/23/16686532/surgeon-mistakes-gender-wage-gap.
15. Ashleigh Shelby Rosette and Robert W. Livingston, "Failure Is Not an Option for Black Women: Effects of Organizational Performance on Leaders with Single Versus Dual-Subordinate Identities," *Journal of Experimental Social Psychology* 48, no. 5 (2012): 1162–1167, https://doi.org/10.1016/j.jesp.2012.05.002.
16. Thekla Morgenroth et al., "The Gendered Consequences of Risk-Taking at Work: Are Women Averse to Risk or to Poor Consequences?" *Psychology of Women Quarterly* 46, no. 3 (2022): 257–277, https://doi.org/10.1177/03616843221084048.
17. Fiona Macaulay and Deborah Riegel, "Fear of Failure in Professional & Personal Life Research Insights," survey conducted April 2024.

CHAPTER 3

1. Brené Brown, *The Gifts of Imperfection: Let Go of Who You Think You're Supposed to Be and Embrace Who You Are* (Hazelden, 2010), 7.
2. Brown, *The Gifts of Imperfection*, 56.
3. Bart Soenens et al., "The Intergenerational Transmission of Perfectionism: Parents' Psychological Control as an Intervening Variable," *Journal of Family Psychology* 19, no. 3 (2005): 358–366, https://doi.org/10.1037/0893-3200.19.3.358.
4. Di Wu et al., "Perfectionism Mediated the Relationship Between Brain Structure Variation and Negative Emotion in a Nonclinical Sample," *Cognitive, Affective, & Behavioral Neuroscience* 17 (2017): 211–223, https://doi.org/10.3758/s13415-016-0474-8.
5. Heidi Grant Halvorson, "The Trouble with Bright Girls," *Psychology Today*, January 27, 2011, https://www.psychologytoday.com/us/blog/the-science-of-success/201101/the-trouble-with-bright-girls.
6. Thomas Curran and Andrew P. Hill, "Perfectionism Is Increasing Over Time: A Meta-Analysis of Birth Cohort Differences from 1989 to 2016," *Psychological Bulletin* 145, no. 4 (2019): 410–429, https://doi.org/10.1037/bul0000138.
7. Christia Spears Brown and The Conversation US, "Here's Why States Are Suing Meta for Hurting Teens with Facebook and Instagram," *Scientific American*, October 26, 2023, https://www.scientificamerican.com/article/heres-why-states-are-suing-meta-for-hurting-teens-with-facebook-and-instagram/.

8. Kara Alaimo, *Over the Influence: Why Social Media Is Toxic for Women and Girls—and How We Can Take It Back* (Alcove Press, 2024), Introduction.
9. Leah A. Plunkett, *Sharenthood: Why We Should Think Before We Talk About Our Kids Online* (The MIT Press, 2019), quoted in Alaimo, p 12.
10. Fiona Macaulay and Deborah Riegel, "Fear of Failure in Professional & Personal Life Research Insights," survey conducted April 2024.
11. Tara Sophia Mohr, "Why Women Don't Apply for Jobs Unless They're 100% Qualified," *Harvard Business Review*, August 25, 2014, https://hbr.org/2014/08/why-women-dont-apply-for-jobs-unless-theyre-100-qualified.
12. SHRM (Society for Human Resource Management), "Just 13% of Women Promote Their Success and Accomplishments to Their Leaders and Peers . . .," LinkedIn, August 1, 2023. https://www.linkedin.com/posts/linkage-inc-_how-women-leaders-can-tell-their-story-of-activity-7070043858104918019-Bk75.
13. Sarah Chen-Spellings, "Mistakes Are the Greatest Teachers—If You're Willing to Learn from Them," LinkedIn, https://www.linkedin.com/posts/mistakes-are-the-great-activity-7284936496489328642-MkNL/.
14. Juliet Wairimu, "The Maverick Mind of Steve Jobs," *Journal*, 2023, accessed June 5, 2025, https://vocal.media/journal/the-maverick-mind-of-steve-jobs.
15. Lou Holtz, *Winning Every Day: The Game Plan for Success* (Harper Business, 1998), xvi.

CHAPTER 4

1. Fiona Macaulay and Deborah Riegel, "Fear of Failure in Professional & Personal Life Research Insights," survey conducted April 2024.
2. Paola Cecchi-Dimeglio, "How Gender Bias Corrupts Performance Reviews, and What to Do About It," *Harvard Business Review*, April 12, 2017, https://hbr.org/2017/04/how-gender-bias-corrupts-performance-reviews-and-what-to-do-about-it.
3. Shelley J. Correll and Caroline Simard, "Research: Vague Feedback Is Holding Women Back," *Harvard Business Review*, April 29, 2016, https://hbr.org/2016/04/research-vague-feedback-is-holding-women-back.
4. Amy Diehl, Leanne M. Dzubinski, and Amber L. Stephenson, "New Research Reveals the 30 Critiques Holding Women Back from Leadership That Most Men Will Never Hear," *Fast Company*, May 2, 2023, https://www.fastcompany.com/90889985/new-research-reveals-critiques-holding-women-back-from-leadership-that-most-men-will-never-hear.
5. Amelia Costigan, "The Double-Bind Dilemma for Women in Leadership," *Catalyst Insights*, February 16, 2024, https://www.catalyst.org/insights/2024/infographic-the-double-bind-dilemma-for-women-in-leadership.
6. Catherine H. Tinsley and Robin J. Ely, "What Most People Get Wrong About Men and Women," *Harvard Business Review*, May–June 2018, https://hbr.org/2018/05/what-most-people-get-wrong-about-men-and-women.

7. Kieran Snyder, *The Abrasiveness Trap*, Stanford University, 2014, https://web.stanford.edu/dept/radiology/cgi-bin/raddiversity/wp-content/uploads/2017/12/TheAbrasivenessTrap.pdf.
8. Kristen Parisi, "Race and Gender Stereotypes Permeate in Performance Reviews, Study Finds," *HR Brew*, August 26, 2024, https://www.hr-brew.com/stories/2024/08/26/race-and-gender-stereotypes-permeate-in-performance-reviews-study-finds.
9. Merrit Stüven, "The Role of Gender and Race in Performance Appraisals," Harvard Kennedy School, Women and Public Policy Program, September 20, 2021, https://www.hks.harvard.edu/centers/wappp/news-and-events/role-gender-and-race-performance-appraisals.
10. Janelle Nanos, "Why Women Fall into the Negative Feedback Trap," *The Boston Globe*, October 23, 2018, https://www.bostonglobe.com/magazine/2018/10/23/why-women-fall-into-negative-feedback-trap/d4pacw1hnLz1MJ24UzsigJ/story.html.

CHAPTER 5

1. Chloe Malle, "Inside Dating-App Bumble's Bid for Global Domination," *Vogue*, April 18, 2019, https://www.vogue.com/article/bumble-india-whitney-wolfe-herd-interview-may-2019-issue.
2. Charlotte Alter, "How Whitney Wolfe Herd Turned a Vision of a Better Internet Into a Billion-Dollar Brand," *Time*, March 19, 2021, https://time.com/5947727/whitney-wolfe-herd-bumble/.
3. Taylor Locke, "Bumble CEO Whitney Wolfe Herd on Achieving Success," CNBC Make It, February 11, 2021, https://www.cnbc.com/2021/02/11/bumble-ceo-whitney-wolfe-herd-on-achieving-success.html.
4. Locke, "Bumble CEO Whitney Wolfe Herd on Achieving Success."
5. "Bumble CEO Whitney Wolfe Herd On Empowering Women To Make The First Move," *ForbesWomen*, May 18, 2021, https://www.bing.com/videos/riverview/relatedvideo?q=who+is+respomibsble+for+the+women+make+the+first+move+philosophy+of+Bumble&mid=2A94289EA447587975C32A94289EA447587975C3&FORM=VIRE.
6. Alter, "How Whitney Wolfe Herd Turned a Vision of a Better Internet Into a Billion-Dollar Brand."
7. Sarah Todd, "Bumble Founder Whitney Wolfe Herd Discusses Her Return as CEO," *Fortune*, March 26, 2025, https://fortune.com/2025/03/26/bumble-whitney-wolfe-herd-founder-back-as-ceo-interview-love-company/.
8. Todd, "Bumble Founder Whitney Wolfe Herd Discusses Her Return as CEO."
9. Todd, "Bumble Founder Whitney Wolfe Herd Discusses Her Return as CEO."
10. Interview with Fiona Macaulay, November 18, 2023.
11. Matthew Lieberman, *Social: Why Our Brains Are Wired to Connect* (Crown Publishers, 2013).
12. Deborah Grayson Riegel and Scott Doyle interview of Frances Frei, October 17, 2023.

13. Brené Brown, *Daring Greatly: How the Courage to Be Vulnerable Transforms the Way We Live, Love, Parent, and Lead* (Gotham Books, 2012), 34–36, 45–46.

CHAPTER 6

1. Melanie Perkins, "21 Questions from Aussie Startups: Highs, Lows & Lessons Learned During Canva's Journey So Far (Part 1)," Canva Newsroom, January 13, 2018, https://www.canva.com/newsroom/news/melanie-perkins-21-questions-part-1/.
2. Perkins, "21 Questions from Aussie Startups."
3. Denham Sadler, "How Canva Co-Founder Melanie Perkins Overcame Rejection to Build a 'Truly Stunning' Startup," *SmartCompany*, May 26, 2016, https://www.smartcompany.com.au/growth/canva-founder-melanie-perkins-overcame-rejection-build-truly-stunning-startup.
4. "The Top 20 Reasons Startups Fail," CB Insights, 2019, https://www.cbinsights.com/research/startup-failure-reasons-top/.
5. "Figma Rival Canva Valued at $42bn as IPO Rumours Swirl," *Financial Times*, August 20, 2025, https://www.ft.com/content/fbf2c84c-81bd-4349-88ca-efbff5fb3c89.
6. Andrew Beattie, "Why Did Pets.com Crash So Drastically?" *Investopedia*, updated October 31, 2021, https://www.investopedia.com/ask/answers/08/dotcom-pets-dot-com.asp.
7. Joshua Bote, "Pets.com Was an SF Sensation. It Collapsed Months After Going Public," *SFGate*, July 18, 2023, https://www.sfgate.com/tech/article/pets-dot-com-sock-puppet-look-back-18205346.php.
8. Catherine Clifford, "It's Never Too Late to Succeed: How This 60-Year-Old Founder Took Her Business from Zero to $500 Million in 6 Years," CNBC, July 20, 2017, https://www.cnbc.com/2017/07/20/a-60-year-old-entrepreneur-took-her-business-from-zero-to-500-million.html.
9. "Julie Wainwright," The Mollie Plotkin Group, https://mollieplotkingroup.com/speaker/julie-wainwright/.
10. Dori Zinn, "After Failure Comes Finding Yourself—Julie Wainwright on Authenticity, Alignment, and the Environment," *HerMoney*, September 6, 2023, https://hermoney.com/earn/julie-wainwright-the-real-real-female-founder/.
11. Zinn, "After Failure Comes Finding Yourself."

CHAPTER 7

1. Rosemary Feitelberg, "Intrepid Fashion Editor Polly Mellen Dies at 100," *Women's Wear Daily*, December 12, 2024, https://wwd.com/eye/people/vogue-fashion-editor-polly-mellen-dies-1236763425/.

2. Jean Li Spencer, "Venerable Vera," *ELYSIAN Magazine*, November 2, 2022, https://readelysian.com/venerable-vera/.
3. Jade Scipioni, "Designer Vera Wang on Starting Her Company at 40," CNBC Make It, updated May 20, 2021, https://www.cnbc.com/2021/05/18/vera-wang-on-starting-her-company-at-40-.html.
4. "Vera Wang," *Britannica*, August 10, 2022, https://www.britannica.com/biography/Vera-Wang.
5. Lisa Lockwood, "Vera Wang's Fashion Brand Sold to WHP Global," *Women's Wear Daily*, December 16, 2024, https://wwd.com/business-news/markets/vera-wang-fashion-brand-ip_sold-whp-global-1236767014/.
6. Scipioni, "Designer Vera Wang on Starting Her Company at 40."
7. Katty Kay and Claire Shipman, *The Confidence Code: The Science and Art of Self-Assurance—What Women Should Know* (Harper Business, 2014).
8. Carol S. Dweck, *The Power of Yet* (video, November 2014), TEDxNorrköping.
9. Frances Frei, in *Building Trust for Cultural Change* with Dr. Diane Hamilton (podcast interview, 2018).
10. Abhishek Parajuli, "The Punishment Gap: How Workplace Mistakes Hurt Women and Minorities Most," *World Economic Forum*, June 18, 2019, citing Mark Egan et al.'s working paper; see also "Women Surgeons Are Punished More Than Men for the Exact Same Mistakes," *Vox*, November 23, 2017.
11. Amy C. Edmondson, *The Fearless Organization: Creating Psychological Safety in the Workplace for Learning, Innovation, and Growth* (Wiley, 2019), 13.
12. Deborah A. O'Neil and Diana Bilimoria, "Women's Career Development Phases: Idealism, Endurance, and Reinvention," *Career Development International* 10, no. 3 (2005): 168–189. https://doi.org/10.1108/13620430510598300.
13. Joan C. Williams and Rachel Dempsey, *What Works for Women at Work: Four Patterns Working Women Need to Know* (NYU Press, 2014), 192–195.
14. Juliet Eilperin, "White House Women Want to Be in the Room Where It Happens," *The Washington Post*, September 13, 2016, https://www.washingtonpost.com/news/powerpost/wp/2016/09/13/white-house-women-want-to-be-in-the-room-where-it-happens/.
15. Jessica Bennett, "On Campus, Failure Is on the Syllabus," *The New York Times*, June 24, 2017, https://www.nytimes.com/2017/06/24/fashion/fear-of-failure.html.
16. Bennett, "On Campus, Failure Is on the Syllabus."
17. Scott Doyle interview of Rachel Simmons, December 9, 2023.

CHAPTER 8

1. Reshma Saujani, *Brave, Not Perfect: Fear Less, Fail More, and Live Bolder* (Crown Currency, 2019), 203.
2. Saujani, *Brave, Not Perfect*, 147.

3. Elena Greguletz, Marjo-Riitta Diehl, and Karin Kreutzer, "Why Women Build Less Effective Networks Than Men: The Role of Structural Exclusion and Personal Hesitation," *Human Relations* 72, no. 7 (2019): 1234–1261, https://doi.org/10.1177/0018726718804303.
4. Bonita Stewart and Jacqueline Adams, *A Blessing: Women of Color Teaming Up to Lead, Empower and Thrive* (Wordeee, 2020), 148–155.
5. Rob Cross, Inga Carboni, and Jessica Huang, "The Relational Analytics of Organizational Potential: Diagnosing and Mobilizing Networks for Collaboration and Innovation," *Organizational Dynamics* 48, no. 3 (2019): 47–55.
6. Laura Rua-Gomez et al., "Building Professional Networks: A Systematic Review of Interventions to Enhance Career Success," *Journal of Vocational Behavior* 151 (2024): 103922.

PART 3: BOUNCE BACK

1. Amy Morin, "10 Healthy Ways to Cope with Failure," *Verywell Mind*, updated November 8, 2024, https://www.verywellmind.com/healthy-ways-to-cope-with-failure-4163968.
2. Noelle Nelson et al., "Emotions Know Best: The Advantage of Emotional Versus Cognitive Responses to Failure," *Journal of Behavioral Decision Making* 31, no. 1 (2017): 40–51, https://doi.org/10.1002/bdm.2042.

CHAPTER 9

1. Elizabeth Gilbert, "Your Elusive Creative Genius," TED Talk, February 2009.
2. Elizabeth Gilbert, *Big Magic: Creative Living Beyond Fear* (Riverhead Books, 2015). And Elizabeth Gilbert, interview by Oprah Winfrey, "Super Soul Sunday," OWN: Oprah Winfrey Network, October 5, 2014.
3. Doug O'Brien, "Self Hypnosis: 'The Betty Erickson Special,'" *Ericksonian*, March 4, 2017, https://ericksonian.info/therapeutic_scripts/self-hypnosis-the-betty-erickson-special/.
4. Kristin Neff, "What Is Self-Compassion?" *Self-Compassion*, accessed June 6, 2025, https://self-compassion.org/what-is-self-compassion/#the-elements-of-self-compassion.
5. Neff, "What Is Self-Compassion?"
6. University of California—Los Angeles, "Putting Feelings Into Words Produces Therapeutic Effects in the Brain," ScienceDaily, June 22, 2007, www.sciencedaily.com/releases/2007/06/070622090727.htm.
7. Forbes Coaches Council, "14 Ways to Pick Yourself Back Up After a Major Failure," *Forbes*, March 17, 2020, https://www.forbes.com/councils/forbescoachescouncil/2020/03/17/14-ways-to-pick-yourself-back-up-after-a-major-failure/.
8. Gertrude Himmelfarb, *The De-Moralization of Society: From Victorian Virtues to Modern Values* (Vintage, 1995), 10.

9. "How and Why Does Misinformation Spread?" American Psychological Association, updated March 1, 2024, https://www.apa.org/topics/journalism-facts/how-why-misinformation-spreads.
10. Soroush Vosoughi et al., "The Spread of True and False News Online," *Science* 359, no. 6380 (2018): 1146–1151, https://doi.org/10.1126/science.aap9559.
11. Mary-Frances O'Connor, *The Grieving Brain: The Surprising Science of How We Learn from Love and Loss* (HarperOne, 2022), 24–25.
12. Bruce D. Perry and Oprah Winfrey, *What Happened to You? Conversations on Trauma, Resilience, and Healing* (Flatiron Books, 2021).
13. David Kessler, *Finding Meaning: The Sixth Stage of Grief* (Scribner, 2020), 6–8.
14. John Elfers et al., "Resilience and Loss: The Correlation of Grief and Gratitude," *International Journal of Applied Positive Psychology* 9 (2024): 327–345, https://doi.org/10.1007/s41042-023-00126-1.

CHAPTER 10

1. Patricia Obiero quotations from an interview with FailLab.
2. Daniel Pink, *The Power of Regret* (Riverhead Books, 2022), 54.
3. Pink, *The Power of Regret*.
4. Fiona Macaulay's interview of Tine Knott, November 29, 2023.
5. Maika Leibbrandt, "How to Talk About Failure: Strengths and Our Weak Moments," Gallup CliftonStrengths, March 31, 2016, https://www.gallup.com/cliftonstrengths/en/250802/talk-failure-strengths-weak-moments.aspx.
6. Adam Grant, "Bouncing Back from Rejection," LinkedIn, April 22, 2019, https://www.linkedin.com/pulse/bouncing-back-from-rejection-adam-grant/.
7. Marion Eberly et al., "It's Not Me, It's Not You, It's Us! An Empirical Examination of Relational Attributions," *Journal of Applied Psychology* 102, no. 5 (2017): 711–731, https://doi.org/10.1037/apl0000187.
8. Suzy Welch, "The Rule of 10-10-10," Oprah.com, accessed June 6, 2025, https://www.oprah.com/spirit/suzy-welchs-rule-of-10-10-10-decision-making-guide/all.
9. Brian Uzzi, "Research: Men and Women Need Different Kinds of Networks to Succeed," *Harvard Business Review*, February 25, 2019, https://hbr.org/2019/02/research-men-and-women-need-different-kinds-of-networks-to-succeed.
10. Tim Bower, "The Secrets of Successful Female Networkers," *Harvard Business Review*, November–December 2019, https://hbr.org/2019/11/the-secrets-of-successful-female-networkers.
11. Michael Lewis, *The Premonition: A Pandemic Story* (W. W. Norton, 2021).
12. Robert Kegan and Lisa Laskow Lahey, *Immunity to Change: How to Overcome It and Unlock the Potential in Yourself and Your Organization* (Harvard Business Review Press, 2009), 45–52.
13. Tasha Eurich, *Insight: The Surprising Truth About How Others See Us, How We See*

Ourselves, and Why the Answers Matter More Than We Think* (Crown Business, 2017), 4–6.

14. Tasha Eurich, "What Self-Awareness Really Is (and How to Cultivate It)," *Harvard Business Review*, January 4, 2018, https://hbr.org/2018/01/what-self-awareness-really-is-and-how-to-cultivate-it.
15. Junot Díaz, "Apocalypse: What Disasters Reveal," *Boston Review*, May/June 2011, https://bostonreview.net/articles/junot-diaz-apocalypse-disaster-capitalism/.
16. Eurich, *Insight*, 44.
17. *Black Panther*, directed by Ryan Coogler (Marvel Studios, 2018).

CHAPTER 11

1. *Losers*, episode 1, "Surya Bonaly," directed by Mickey Duzyj, Netflix, March 1, 2019.
2. *Losers*, episode 1.
3. Shattuck-St. Mary's, "Former Olympian Surya Bonaly Joins Shattuck-St. Mary's Figure Skating Coaching Staff," June 6, 2024, https://www.s-sm.org/news-events/news/~board/school-news/post/former-olympian-surya-bonaly-joins-shattuck-st-marys-figure-skating-coaching-staff.
4. Amy C. Edmondson, *Right Kind of Wrong: The Science of Failing Well* (Atria Books, 2023), 19.
5. From FailLab talk delivered in 2021.
6. Shlomo Sprung, "Mickey Duzyj Discusses His Netflix Sports Documentary Series 'Losers,' and How Athletes Deal with Their Biggest Failures," *Awful Announcing*, February 28, 2019, awfulannouncing.com/netflix/mickey-duzyj-discusses-his-netflix-sports-documentary-series-losers.html.
7. Zachary Petit, "Micky Duzyj Animates His Way to Two Emmy Nods with 'Losers,'" *PRINT*, August 10, 2020, https://www.printmag.com/designer-interviews/mickey-duzyj-animates-his-way-to-two-emmy-nods-with-losers/.
8. Tina Fey, *Bossypants* (Reagan Arthur Books, 2011), 123.
9. Deborah Grayson Riegel and Sophie Riegel, *Go to Help: 31 Strategies to Offer, Ask For, and Accept Help* (Panoma Press, 2022), 100.
10. "The Science of Celebration: How Celebrating Boosts Happiness and Well-Being," *New York Trend*, June 2, 2023, https://newyorktrendnyc.com/2023/06/the-science-of-celebration-how-celebrating-boosts-happiness-and-well-being/.
11. Judith E. Glaser, *Conversational Intelligence: How Great Leaders Build Trust and Get Extraordinary Results* (Routledge, 2016), 115–117.
12. Austa Somvichian-Clausen, "Two Women in STEM Investigate the Science Behind Celebration," *The Hill*, December 1, 2020, https://thehill.com/changing-america/well-being/mental-health/528245-two-women-in-stem-investigate-the-science-behind/.

13. BJ Fogg, "How You Can Use the Power of Celebration to Make New Habits Stick," Ideas.TED.com, January 6, 2020, https://ideas.ted.com/how-you-can-use-the-power-of-celebration-to-make-new-habits-stick/.
14. Catherine Moore, "What Is Negativity Bias and How Can It Be Overcome?" PositivePsychology.com, December 30, 2019, https://positivepsychology.com/3-steps-negativity-bias/#:~text=Negativity%20bias%20helps%20them%20avoid,useful%20as%20it%20once%20was.

About the Authors

ABOUT DEBORAH GRAYSON RIEGEL

Deb is an executive coach, keynote speaker, workshop facilitator, and consultant who helps leaders and teams communicate with less stress and greater successes. She has been an instructor of leadership communication at the Wharton School of the University of Pennsylvania, Columbia Business School's Women in Leadership Program, and Duke's Fuqua School of Business. She writes for *Harvard Business Review*, *Psychology Today*, and *Inc.* and is the author of (now) ten books on leadership, communication, and mental well-being. Deb and her husband, Michael, live in Chapel Hill, North Carolina, and are the proud parents of twins, Jacob and Sophie, and their rescue pit bull, Nash. When Deb isn't working, she is traveling, cooking, reading, and singing show tunes out loud.

Learn more: www.DeborahGraysonRiegel.com
Deb@DeborahGraysonRiegel.com

ABOUT FIONA M. MACAULAY

Fiona is an entrepreneur, keynote speaker, workshop facilitator, and executive coach who helps Fortune 500 leaders transform failure into competitive advantage through resilience and strategic risk-taking. She is the founder and CEO of the award-winning Women for Impactful Leadership Development (WILD) Network, connecting twenty-five thousand leaders across one hundred countries, and serves as professor and entrepreneur-in-residence at Georgetown University's McDonough School of Business. Recognized among the top 1 percent of women entrepreneurs in the United States and honored by Thinkers50, Fiona has been featured in *The New York Times*, *Fortune*, and *Oprah* magazine and serves on boards, including Junior Achievement Worldwide. Fiona and her husband live in Washington, DC, and are the proud parents of their daughters. When Fiona isn't transforming leaders or building impactful organizations, she is leading Next Chapter walking retreats and working to maintain her competitive tennis game.

Learn more: www.FionaMacaulay.com
Fiona@FionaMacaulay.com

Download your free Personal Board of Directors Builder at
www.FionaMacaulay.com/BoardBuilder

www.ingramcontent.com/pod-product-compliance
Lightning Source LLC
LaVergne TN
LVHW040057080526
838202LV00045B/3683